MODERN SHOW JUMPING

Great Britain—Marion Mould on Stroller

MODERN SHOW JUMPING

COUNT ILIAS TOPTANI

New York

Published by ARCO PUBLISHING COMPANY, Inc.
219 Park Avenue South, New York, N.Y. 10003

First Arco Printing, 1973
First published 1954
Revised edition 1967
New Revised edition 1972

Library of Congress Catalog Card Number 73-76414
ISBN 0-668-02796-7 (cloth)
ISBN 0-668-03334-7 (paper)

Printed in the United States of America

CONTENTS

5

ILLUSTRATIONS

PHOTOGRAPHS

LINE DRAWINGS

In the Text

In the Appendices

FOREWORD

By BRIGADIER J. C. FRIEDBERGER, D.S.O.

It is refreshing to read a book on show jumping written from a new angle. Here we have an invigorating wind blowing from South America, from countries where riding clubs abound and where horses are inexpensive; where you can ride when you like, whoever you are, and without many of the difficulties that face us in Britain today.

Show jumping is highly competitive. Many sports and games you can go on enjoying without ever being very good at them; you may hunt or play polo reasonably well with continuous benefit, interest and amusement. But racing and show jumping will not give you much fun unless you occasionally win or are placed.

This book points to the ingredients of success: to understand the temperament and mechanics of the horse; to train both horse and rider in sensible stages; to enter in suitable classes at the right stage of training. Above all, you and your horse must go into the ring in the proper frame of mind.

The author's experience is firmly based on long years of apprenticeship in the saddle and many successes in the show ring. He has travelled widely and made sound deductions from the exploits of many international horsemen. With these he has coupled the knowledge that comes to us down many centuries of horsemanship from the days of Xenophon and Alexander.

Count Toptani is refreshingly forthright in his opinions. He is no advocate of deliberately placing a horse at his fence; that is the horse's job, the result of training and experience. He is a firm believer in sustained momentum derived from speed on the approach. Loose jumping and all work at liberty have no place in his curriculum. He gives full reasons, and it is open to the reader to agree, to refute or to compromise.

In the chapters that follow, the amateur of today, whether novice or master, will find much that will guide him to early or further success.

Chapter One

Horsemanship

Show jumping originated in England like almost every sport—England being undoubtedly the home of all sports, especially those connected with horses. Even polo, an oriental game originally, was introduced to the Western world by English sportsmen. England, Ireland and the United States even specialised in the first horse to be used for sport—the hunter. The English and Irish are decidedly the best judges of horse-flesh and have shown to the entire horse-world how horses should best be cared for. Even the horse-box is of English origin. Whereas even today horses are still tied up in stalls, the English horse lovers have been using loose boxes for over a hundred and fifty years.

The best saddlery used to be produced in England. Most horsemen still insist that the best boots and smartest breeches can only be obtained in England. English and Irish horse-vets are still everywhere considered the best and English and Irish farriers are unequalled and are the most difficult to obtain. More men, women and children ride in England for pleasure than anywhere else in the world, where riding is still considered a luxury sport or a simple means of transportation.

In its beginning even show jumping was nothing but a condensed sort of the English hunting-field, allowing non-riders to watch the brave horsemen negotiating formidable obstacles, whilst they themselves sat in comfort in sheltered tribunes. In those early beginnings the courses consisted of six to eight obstacles scattered indifferently over a wide area, showing the public what hurdles the valiant huntsman encountered in a hunting field. Even today our modern obstacles bare names reminiscent of the English hunting-field, such as hedge, hogsback, post and rails, etc. There were horse-shows and jumping events in England long before this exciting sport ever reached the Continent, and, ever since, show riding has become every year more and more popular.

Although I have heard it prophesied many times since the end of the last war that horse-sports were doomed, a thing of the past, like so many other Victorian sports, quite the contrary has actually happened. Whereas before the war only a very small and privileged minority seemed to participate in equestrian sports, there are literally thousands of fresh enthusiasts joining every year the ever increasing equestrian fraternity. On the other hand, polo and racing seem to me to lose every year more and more followers.

Since practically all the cavalry regiments in the world have been mechanised, and hence the old-established remount centres have been closed, it is undoubtedly due to the new popularity of show jumping that our beloved friend, the horse, has stayed alive and has not become just a thing of the past to be seen in archaeological museums only. To begin with the closing of the famous cavalry training centres has had also a most fortunate result—experienced cavalry instructors, with nothing better to do, have dedicated themselves to the training of civilians. I have personally seen and visited hundreds of such new civilian training centres for horse lovers which have sprung up since the last war and I can truthfully state that thanks to many of those centres our favourite sport has not only survived but has gained thousands of new adherants throughout the world.

Those experienced cavalry instructors had to adapt themselves very soon to a civilian life and to civilian ways. Their
tuition methods, I noticed, became more supple, old-fashioned
and rigid principles were dropped and were replaced with modern
methods, more suitable to civilians. But the fundamental cavalry
principles of training were wisely maintained, even if the main
emphasis was placed on a most important factor—safety! In
none of the hundreds of such riding centres did I find that old-
fashioned cavalry idea, that youngsters must learn the hard way,
fall often and get hurt so as to become tough. I don't think I am
mistaken when I state that the great popularity of show jumping
is in parts, at least, due to this new tendency, certainly as far as the
parents of the young riders are concerned.

I have always emphasised this as the basis of all equestrian
sports, and I still maintain that this wonderful sport and the
training for it should be made as safe as possible for the young
beginners. I can also fully understand that the parents appreciate
this tendency to maximum safety for their children, for, after all,
they want their youngsters to enjoy the sport and improve their
standard with a minimum of relative danger attached to it.
Watching such jumping events ought to be an enjoyable event
for the parents, and not a nerve-shaking experience.

Whatever my German friends may say of the great interest in
dressage riding, it is jumping that has attracted the ever increasing
interest of the public at large. Without the paying public I have
been assured that show jumping events would soon become what
they were before the war, a sophisticated gathering of a select
few, watching with mild interest the brave endeavours of a few
valiant riders over a few obstacles, playing polo or indulging in
that refined art of horsemanship, dressage.

I personally must admit, that in many ways I loved those times
but then I must forget my nostalgia as what we are concerned with
is being able to support economically our favourite sport. In
short, Modern Show Jumping with all its loudness, its gaudiness,
its excited and yelling crowds of spectators has come to stay.

Without its crowds of spectators, the thrifty horse breeders throughout the world would soon stop breeding horses, as they would then not get the high prices for their products they are getting today and show jumping would become a thing of the past.

However in my many recent visits to riding centres throughout Europe I have discovered to my regret that a small proportion of these ex-cavalry instructors who still survive continue to teach the old-fashioned methods of their cavalry schools. They have made little effort to adapt to modern methods, and consequently their schools are not in keeping with the requirements of our jumping events today. They are simply perpetuating methods and ways which died elsewhere at the time when the old cavalry schools closed down over 30 years ago! I cannot condemn here strongly enough such utter lack of common sense. The worst thing a riding teacher can possibly do is to advise his pupils to try and emulate the ways in which those champion riders have achieved their great successes! I want to refute here right away the general belief that a first-class sportsman is automatically also a first class instructor of his sport! The reason I fear is that these instructors were never themselves taught to teach HOW to jump, so neither could these instructors teach others to jump; what they have done is to adopt the next best subterfuge, advocating methods and a style by which those few natural riders achieved their successes.

On the other hand it is only fair to say that there is now a far greater awareness of the value of correct instruction. Only recently, in fact, an international convention was held at the British Horse Society's National Equestrian Centre at Stoneleigh, Warwickshire under the auspices of the Federation Equestre Internationale for the purpose of discussing the training and supply of instructors.

In Great Britain, particularly, despite the recognised shortage of instructors in comparison with the number of people wanting to learn to ride, there are a number of very good schools where

France—Monsieur J. P. D'Oriola, Gold Medallist at the 1964 Olympic Games

Captain d'Inzeo, Italy

Germany—Herr H. G. Winkler

jumping is taught well; frequently it must be admitted, by young ladies who, whilst basing their instruction on established precepts, are anything but hide-bound traditionalists.

In France, too, the French Federation of Equestrian Sports is reorganising on a pattern similar to that employed in Great Britain, the country being divided into regions, and is making serious attempts to raise the level of instruction within proved modern principles.

Whilst in other European countries there still remain a few of the old-type instructors I have mentioned their influence must, in the way of nature, be waning. There is really no place now for the riding instructor who makes a youngster trot with two large coins placed under his knees as was the fashion when I had my first cavalry lessons 50 years ago.

To teach in this way is to ignore the most elementary conditions of a correct jumping seat. All the pupils learn is to hold on for dear life with their knees, *pivoting on one small point,* instead of gripping strongly, first of all with their calves, then with their thighs and last of all with their *knees.* The knees, of course, only come into the picture *after* the jump, when the horse is landing. I shall come back to this all-important grip in jumping in the chapter on the modern seat.

A final point about those champion riders. It should be remembered that the half-dozen top riders may have at their disposal at the start of the season a whole string of horses of which, for a variety of reasons, only two or three will actually participate in big events.

Obviously, it is far easier under these circumstances to finish up with a champion horse than if you start out with but a single animal. Beginners, therefore, are best advised to learn the correct way to sit, to jump and to ride in a modern seat and forget about the acrobatics or methods employed by those admired champions, who are usually, as I said, natural riders.

Just as show jumping originated in England, another innovation has originated there—the female groom! When last in

England, after years of absence, I discovered that that well-known old character the stable-lad had to all purpose disappeared. Everything in English stables was done by young girls and most efficiently at that. It was explained to me that they were all pupils who thus served their apprenticeship in stable management. An excellent idea, I thought, but impossible to apply, unfortunately, in Continental countries where our dainty young women would be horrified at the mere idea of grooming their horses—to say nothing of carting out the manure! I was quite impressed by the efficiency of those young girls, but mostly by their toughness. I have seen them being kicked and bitten by horses without once really complaining. Most men have always had an erroneous impression about English girls in general and the horsey type in particular—we imagined them to be very tall and anaemic looking. I did not find one such girl in all England. They were all—if I may say so—shockingly healthy! Young Amazons! I watched them ride and take bad falls, only to climb back immediately into the saddle and carry on.

When one of our young women falls off she is usually put on a stretcher and sent home in an ambulance, and she remains in bed for at least a week—if only to receive the visits of her friends and to be able to explain again and again in full detail the whole dreadful ordeal and the appalling sufferings she has had to endure, while languishing in lovely *déshabillé*, perfumed and surrounded by flowers sent by admirers. (I wonder which of the two is right from the masculine point of view?)

THE OLD CAVALRY CENTRES

At the beginning of the last war most cavalry schools closed down. With them died an old and cherished tradition, giving way to modernisation and mechanisation. Hanover was closed down and Saumur, too; Tor di Quinto closed its doors and so did Fort Riley, Kansas—even Weedon, which had produced the fine English cavalrymen, closed down.

Today there are only a few such military training centres left open, most of them in South America, one in Turkey and in Iran, I believe, and the Cavalry School of Madrid. The Argentine still keeps several cavalry regiments mounted. The very nature of the country, its wide, endless plains crossed only by very soft country roads, which invariably turn into bottomless mud tracks with the first winter rains, make the horse the only means of transportation.

In the Campo de Mayo (Buenos Aires), where most military establishments are concentrated, there is one of the finest cavalry training grounds in the world, with miles and miles of undulating grounds, natural and semi-natural obstacles and well-planned hurdle lanes and obstacle fields. Every year the army stages its autumn manœuvres, where the cavalry regiments play a great part, especially, as I have said earlier, if the rains have already started.

Chile also still has one or two squadrons, I believe, and Brazil several cavalry regiments. The only other American country with cavalry is Mexico, where conditions, although the reverse of those prevailing in the Argentine, make the horse a necessity. Hence the high standard of the Mexican horsemen.

The Argentinian army used to encourage cavalry officers to take part in all horse events, allowing them to keep up to eight horses or polo ponies each in the squadron stables. Usually they even managed to keep a few more. There were also several military polo teams with a pretty high handicap. Two years ago the army team reached the finals, but was defeated by the famous Champion team of Venano Tuerto, a thirty-six-goal team.

The cavalry also trains its own farriers, very luckily for the civilian horsemen. As everywhere else in the world, there is a great scarcity of competent farriers. This seems to be one of the professions about to die out in the world and good men are overworked to such an extent that they have to give up at an early stage, worked to sheer exhaustion. I am afraid that with the last cavalry regiments the experienced farriers will also vanish, at least in the Americas. It isn't so much the work itself but the lack of apprentices willing to learn the trade that is gradually forcing the profession out of existence. The younger men don't seem to have enough patience for the many years of very hard work necessary to learn a difficult trade and, frankly, I can't blame them. Shoeing a horse is about the toughest bodily work I can think of, and shoeing up to fifteen horses a day is killing for the strongest back. In Europe I found the same thing. Every year there are fewer and fewer farriers because the cavalry schools have all closed down.

Although it has no bearing on show jumping I should like to mention here something about France. I want to congratulate Colonel Cavaillé for his magnificent work in saving the horse in the French army—and the finest horse in the world at that— the Anglo-Arab. As everywhere else, the French Ministry of War abolished the use of horses, which numbered some 9,000 in all after the liberation. Colonel Cavaillé, then in charge of the military horse census and the subsequent liquidation, managed to persuade the Minister of Defence to keep on at least a thousand animals by the very ingenious idea of incorporating horses into the realm of sport. He convinced the army authorities that equitation was as much a sport for the young officers of France as football or athletics—and with very sound reason too. He thus obtained permission to keep 300 horses in Fontainebleau to be regularly issued to young cavalry officers, who thus at least remained efficient horsemen. All he did was to submit a small balance sheet of the upkeep of the stables to his superiors by which he proved that the horses stabled there were actually an asset to the army and not an old-fashioned and useless liability. In 1946 it cost the army 60 francs to feed a remount, but Colonel Cavaillé managed to sell manure at 100 francs per head per day to the Parisian mushroom growers! The French are a most logical people—even the high army authorities—and they imme-diately recognised that army horses were a big factor in national recovery—at least in a limited equestrian field for, as far as I know, there is no case in the world's commerce where one can put

one pound's worth of fuel into a machine and get twenty-five
shillings' worth of residue out of it.

Once Colonel Cavaillé had obtained the all-important permission to keep 300 horses for national equestrian sports he gradually
started to convince the authorities that those three hundred
horses could not last for ever and needed a gradual replacing, so
the National Harras, the French breeding centres, were also saved
and taken into the scheme of national sports and half-supported
by the Ministry of Agriculture. He then went one step further.
He issued horses only to those officers who cared for them best
and were truly sincere horsemen. But he also convinced his
young protégés that an officer, being a gentleman, could not
keep prize money. All the prizes won by French officers go automatically into a 'kitty' kept by the Colonel and the officers get only
the equivalent of £50, a year from that kitty for a new pair of boots
and breeches. From the proceeds of manure sales Colonel Cavaillé
was also able practically to rebuild the vast stables of Fontainebleau, almost destroyed by the Germans, and also to pay for the
voyage of French officers abroad to take part in the great international equestrian events. This is why French officers can be seen
today at every important show from Madrid and Lisbon to
Sweden and Dublin and always remain among the winners. I
can't think of a more ingenious and splendid organisation, and I
think every horseman will agree with me.

What a pity that the U.S.A., who were able to pump billions
of dollars every year into war-torn Europe, did not have a
Colonel Cavaillé to save the equestrian section of their famous
cavalry school of Fort Riley, Kansas, which had been producing the
finest horsemen in the world for the last decades. Or is it perhaps
that Americans are not as fond of mushrooms as the French?

I have heard of prodigies in mathematics, music or chess,
but there is no such thing as a born genius in riding. Riding
must be learnt the hard and correct way; there are no short cuts.
The only correct methods are those of the cavalry schools which
are based on the experience of 2,000 years. It is obvious that if

there were any possible short cuts the army would have adopted them, instead of spending the taxpayers' money and their own time in a lengthy systematic training of recruits. As with the troopers, civilians must start off with this all-important dressage. A show rider needs it as much as an acrobatic diver needs a knowledge of swimming. Obviously no diver in his senses would jump from a high diving-board without first learning to swim. This does not imply that he must first become a swimming champion before learning to dive, and neither is it necessary for a show rider to be a master in *haute école* before starting to jump. But as a diver must learn to swim, so must a show jumper learn to ride correctly, and there is no other way of learning to ride correctly but to start off in a closed manège and learn elementary dressage. This has been proved time and again ever since there were cavalry regiments, and nothing has yet been invented to replace it.

EUROPEAN RIDING CENTRES AND ORGANISATIONS

Probably no one country in Europe has been so affected by the extension in riding activity in the post-war years as Great Britain. Prior to the Second World War riding, and particularly hunting, was confined, largely, to those possessing at least reasonable means and was considered to be a country sport.

Today, however, with an ever-increasing number of people enjoying a high standard of living and considerable leisure time, riding is the sport of every section of society and nowhere is it stronger than in the urban areas. The Pony Club, which commenced in pre-war years, has well over 30,000 members spread throughout the whole country and organised in branches which usually, for the sake of convenience nowadays, take their name from the nearest local hunt. Essentially the Pony Club was intended to introduce children to the hunting field but now, whilst the influence still remains, the accent is more upon competitive sport and much stress is laid on the instructional rallies which are held throughout the holiday periods.

Such has been the success of the Pony Club that there are now some 800 branches in various countries other than Britain, all of which are organised on the same lines.

The Pony Club accepts members up to the age of 17 and associates up to 21 and it serves, therefore, as a great reservoir of equestrian talent which is to be found in very few other European countries.

Since the war, too, a new movement has become established in Britain, that of the riding clubs for adults. These clubs are affiliated to the central organisation, the British Horse Society, under the control of which body the Pony Club is also placed. The club movement is now over 300 strong and, whilst not every club has its own facilities, many have the use of training grounds, sometimes of an indoor school, and almost all will have a set of show-jumps.

British riding clubs are not nearly so formal, or indeed, so grand as their European counterparts. In some of them the majority of riders will be horse-owners but in many cases members will have an arrangement to hire horses from local schools.

Schools in Britain are very numerous, indeed, ranging from the humble hacking stable to a number of exceptionally well-equipped establishments where a high standard of tuition is available and where all the necessary facilities are at hand. A great many of these schools operate under the Approval System organised by the British Horse Society and in these cases each one is graded according to the standard of instruction and the facilities available. At the centre of the British riding complex is the B.H.S. National Equestrian Centre at Stoneleigh where the National Instructor presides.

The Centre is a kind of University of the Horse and its principal purpose is to teach instructors from every part of the country. The British authorities calculate that upwards of half a million people ride for pleasure in the British Isles today.

In Britain government finance is available for riding activities and aid can also be obtained from local authorities, but essentially the British scene is dominated by individual enthusiasms and in no country is the interest of the average rider so wide, nor elsewhere is there so much opportunity to take part in competitive horse sports.

Almost every town holds a horse show during the summer months and the calendar of equestrian events between April and October is so full that it would seem difficult to squeeze in even one more fixture in each county. Additionally, show jumping now continues all the year round, competitions being held in various indoor arenas during the winter. Hunting, of course, is in full swing between November and April and is so popular that many packs have had to exclude visitors in order to keep their mounted fields to a reasonable and controllable size.

Outside the hunting areas, and there are a few places in Britain from which a pack of hounds cannot be reached by employing a horse-box or trailer, local riding clubs will organise 'mock' hunts. There is, therefore, a great variety of riding open to British horsemen all the year round, which is not the case in some of the other European countries.

America, too, has its national horse body and, of course, the Pony Club and numerous riding clubs, as well as a large number of fully equipped training centres, particularly on the eastern side of the continent where riding is increasingly popular.

In Germany I was assured that there were more horses and riders than in England but this I find hard to believe and I was unable to obtain from the German Federation an accurate number. Hence I am only repeating here what I was told. I have visited hundreds of riding centres throughout Germany, West Germany that is, and almost a dozen in West Berlin alone. Each of those clubs, and these are not clubs in the sense of those which exist in Britain, could boast of an excellent covered manège, most of them even of Olympic sizes. They all had, also, one or more outdoor manège but for dressage riding only, and nowhere did I find the all important small enclosed manège in which to learn the elementaries of riding. In only a few of those hundreds of riding establishments, with perhaps, indeed, only one exception (Braun-schweig, directed by a first-class man, Herr Rolf Bartels) did I find sufficient grounds devoted exclusively to jumping. Most of the riding establishments had only a most rudimentary and reduced space for those members who wished to learn jumping, with virtually no facilities at all for the young and ambitious show riders. Nowhere did I find what I personally consider an absolute necessity, the jumping-lane with some minimum 10 to 15 obstacles and nowhere did I find so elementary and simple thing as a trotting-lane. When I asked my German friends about this most of them admitted that they had not even heard of such devices (*sic*)!

Everywhere I found that the whole emphasis on riding in Germany was on dressage (dressure as they call it). I daresay that only some 6 to 7 per cent of the German riders dedicated them-selves truly to jumping; the great majority were only interested in dressage at which they truly have become past masters. But this book is about jumping and not about dressage of which I am no judge at all and I should therefore never give an opinion. I still maintain however that this form of training can also be overdone as I noticed everywhere in Germany. After all, a horse and rider should both be trained to be more supple, be more versatile, and a good horse should be able to go over a reasonably low or high course and know something other than simply mak-ing a 'passage', beautiful as this movement of a horse might be.

True, every horse needs a working knowledge of dressage, but only of elementary dressage as I shall explain later on, and I do feel that for an all-round horse over-dressage, if I may call it that, can be as bad as the lack of elementary dressage, which used to be a weakness in England many years ago.

In France I obtained through the good offices of the French Federation a very accurate list of the French riding establishments and the number frankly staggered me! Whereas I knew that there were some dozen or so riding establishments throughout France before the war, there are now over 680 of them. The total of those registered horsemen is over 140,000! I very much doubt whether before the war there were more than 300 dedicated horsemen in all of France, not counting of course the members of the famous French 'Equipages' hunting clubs. In Germany, however, the situation is totally different. By this I mean as far as jumping is concerned. Whereas in Germany the whole emphasis is on dressage riding, in France I would say 80 per cent of the riders are solely interested in jumping. By that I mean that the riding clubs had dedicated 80 per cent or even more of their available space to this activity. I also discovered a most praiseworthy fact, that the French Government automatically granted to all riding clubs a very massive cash subsidy if those riding clubs built a closed manège of Olympic size. Practically all of them had closed manèges when I visited the French centres recently. I want to mention here also one of the latest of such establishments, that of Poitiers in the centre of France. There the provincial authorities used their initiative and had built one of the finest equestrian centres I have had the pleasure of visiting. It had a splendid indoor manège larger by 15 metres than even an Olympic one, the very finest jumping fields and lanes and stables for 150 horses! Many of those horses stabled there also belonged to the Government and the riding teachers were all employed by the Government or local government. This extraordinary interest the French Government has taken in developing the riding sport in France is again, in my opinion, due to the persistent efforts of Colonel Cavaillé, the director of the Fontainebleau School, who immediately after the war convinced the French Government that riding is also a fine sport, at least as fine as football or swimming etc.

I personally believe that the difference in the amount of equestrian activities in Germany and France is mainly due to the available ground in those two countries for equestrian sports. Germany is a highly over-crowded country I discovered— over-crowded in inhabitants and available grounds, whereas France has by far more open ground available.

Nowhere has riding become more popular than in France, that

is post-war France, except in England. In Germany riding is still considered a somewhat exclusive sport, and is out of reach of all but a select minority, but in France and Britain it has become one of *the* most popular sports of all. When taking a taxi last June in Paris to catch the train for Brussels I noticed that the taxi driver had a pair of spurs dangling from his rear-view mirror. When I asked him for the reason he told me quite proudly that his one and only passion in life was horses!

He went on to explain that he would get up at five a.m. in summer so as to get a couple of hours' riding before starting work as a taxi driver in Paris. He also informed me that he had converted two of his friends and the three of them were going to work just for another couple of years at their present jobs—very hard and as much overtime as possible—so as to be able to finish paying off the grounds on which they had an option and on which they were to establish a riding club! He even had half a dozen horses promised to him already by racehorse trainers and thought everything was just perfect till I asked him *who* would do the teaching in his riding club. He almost ran into another cab while thinking over my question. Then he stopped his cab and turning around told me with true innocent apprehension: 'You know, you certainly have brought up a very important point, so important that it is our one and only worry. But then,' he continued, visibly saddened, 'this is *the* main problem in every riding club in France.' He then went on to explain that but for a couple of dozen old cavalry instructors there were only a minute number of ex-top-riders and winners in big shows that taught in France! Even my young taxi driver seemed aware of the one great deficiency in the ever increasing sport of riding, the utter lack of truly competent men who could teach in a modern way and not just carry on from where they had left off before the last world war in 1939! I shall enlarge on this all-important point later on in this book and shall mention here only that this was exactly the same problem I found everywhere in Europe later and which forced me to rewrite completely the chapter on training centres in Europe.

In Belgium I found quite a lot of riding clubs and equestrian centres and was given by the Royal Belgian Equestrian Federation a list of some 1,500 registered show riders; this is quite a lot for so small a country, taking into consideration that at least five times as many riders were not registered with their Federation and only rode for their pleasure and not in shows. In Belgium, as with Holland, I found that rather few such riding clubs could boast of a fairly large-sized indoor manège. Although the weather in Holland and Belgium is anything but sunny, in general, this struck me as rather odd.

All I could think was that apparently the Belgian Minister of Agriculture as with the Dutch one was less generously inclined towards the equestrian sport than his French equivalent. In Switzerland however I found practically the opposite. Although a rather small and very mountainous land, every single riding establishment had an excellent indoor manège, some of them large enough to hold jumping events with up to 13 obstacles. I also met several horsemen who had built their own private indoor manège who kept anything up to eight horses for their pleasure, although some of them never took part in jumping events.

But in Switzerland as in France and Germany there was an obvious lack of competent instructors. In Italy I only discovered a mere half dozen riding establishments. I also was told that there were no more than some 200 to 300 horsemen interested in jumping in the whole of Italy! This surprised me very much as the Italian national team has been and still continues to compete in all international events and consistently finish amongst the leaders. The quality of the Italian riders is apparently kept up by the excellent tradition left by those two great masters and virtual fathers of modern horsemanship, Federico Caprili and Piero Santini. There are, I was told, two or three hunting clubs in Italy, the most important of them in Rome, but otherwise the average Italian was hardly if at all interested in riding himself.

The same I found to be true in Spain. In Madrid there are three first-class riding clubs, the Real Club de Puerta de Hierro, the

Club de la Casa de Campo and the Somasaguas Club. But the main activities of the first mentioned were apparently only culinary. The Real Club prided itself in running a first-class restaurant at quite reasonable prices. It also had the best golf course, in the whole Peninsula but a very mediocre riding section. Most of the riders, stabling there some 130 horses, were simply Sunday riders and the Club offered simply some pleasant riding trails as amenities to its equestrian members.

The Casa de Campo Club which is overburdened with a colossal number of members (17,000 I have been told), specialises more in equestrian activities, which seems to reflect rather badly on its culinary side, but they have one of the finest indoor manège in the whole of Europe, including the show piece of Poitiers. They also have one of the very finest show rings for international events I have seen anywhere in Europe, I daresay even nicer than the famous Piazza de Sienna in the Villa Borghese Park in Rome where all international events are held.

Although the Casa de Campo Club boasts or is burdened with 17,000 members and has raised its entrance fee to equal that of the Club de Puerta de Hierro, probably to keep more horsemen away, I have been assured that there are no more than some 200, if that, registered show riders in Spain. I mean by that true show riders and not merely Sunday riders who could number in all about 1,500.

These naturally do not include the military horsemen who in Spain represent easily 80 per cent of all the participants in show jumping events. Barcelona and the other larger cities naturally also have some quite good riding clubs and there are certainly far more clubs and riders in Spain than in Italy, for all the great difference in population between the two countries. But then Spain has been since medieval times *the* foremost horse-breeding country in Europe. I even unearthed a very curious law which was never actually anulled but only fell in disuse through the centuries: No Hidalgo or Spanish nobleman could ever bestride a mule or a donkey for sport or travelling if he wanted to keep his head on his shoulders! Only women and churchmen were allowed to travel on mules—nobles and cavaliers always had to use horses. Even the oath any caballero of the old religious military orders of Santiago, Calatrave, Alcantara and Montesa had to give was 'that he had never bestridden a mule or donkey even as a child'.

Portugal has several riding clubs and perhaps as many as Italy but I could never obtain any accurate numbers. The majority of the members specialise in jumping and a few in dressage. Though the dressage is excellent, it is in the Spanish traditional style, certainly the oldest in Europe and by far older than German dressage. Its movements are not quite the same as those accepted today in some other countries but it is very much more spectacular. There are also more such centres in Portugal than in Spain and far more enthusiasts. Dressage, as a matter of fact, originated in Spain and Portugal as far back as the 13th and 14th centuries, and was originally brought over, in a form not perhaps recognised today, from Africa by the Moors. Today, even after so many centuries, the original Arab influence in training the Andalusian horses can be seen. The best description I ever heard of such horses was in a delightful book by the most enthusiastic writer about horses, Miss Ursula Bruns which she called *The Dancing Horses of Andalusia*. Andalusian horses as a matter of fact seem to dance more than prance and about the most superb spectacle I can think of is the performance of such Andalusian horses in the bull-ring. To watch such a bull-fight with Portuguese and Spanish *Rejoniadores* (not Picadores, which is quite a different thing and a most pitiful exhibition) mounted on those horses is truly the most spectacular performance I have ever had the privilege to watch. I shall not forget the experience of seeing Angel Peralta galloping straight towards the charging bull without touching his reins and then holding up two very short banderillas, then watching the horse suddenly change all by itself his lead and swerve slightly to the right so that the charging bull shot an inch past its body, thus allowing the rider to plant the banderillas on the bull's neck. Both the Portuguese and the Spanish dressage horses stem originally from the famous *Cartujanos* stallions. I believe these were bred originally, hence their name, in the Charter house of Jerez de los Caballeros. There are also other versions which I shall not enlarge upon as these fabulous horses have nothing to do with the essence of this book!

I was assured that there are quite a number of riding clubs in the northern European countries, Sweden, Norway and Denmark but I was unable to obtain any accurate data on their numbers from the federations of those countries.

THE DIFFERENT HORSE BREEDS

When the first Spanish Conquistadores landed in America the horse was completely unknown. The great initial successes of the Spaniards were mostly due to the element of surprise mingled with the fear the Indians had of those huge four-legged animals which they believed to be part of their riders or vice versa —until they managed to unhorse the first Spaniards.

The origin of the horse in North America can be traced to one roan stallion and five mares left on the banks of the Mississippi by De Soto when he finally decided to abandon his quest for gold in that northerly place, and retreat down the Mississippi on hurriedly made barges.

In South America the horse population was kept up by regular imports of stud animals from Spain, then one of the leading horse-breeding countries in Europe, until today Argentine and Brazil have a horse population of several millions and it is still increasing. The usual South American horse is a short-legged, rather heavy animal with a short neck, big bones and a Roman nose. They all seem to have a certain amount of Percheron blood in them. Contrary to popular belief, Argentina does not breed fine riding horses. The so-called hunter and hack types are completely unknown; only recently did some *estancieros* embark on an ambitious scheme for breeding hunters with more or less success. There is really only one single successful breed in the Argentine, apart from the thoroughbreds, and that is the polo pony. This breed originated from breeding creole mares, which were small but heavy of bone and very tough and used to hard farm work, to thoroughbred stallions. The result was the actual polo pony of today, a small animal with short legs but very fast, sturdy and capable of carrying a lot of weight. The whole success of Argentina's famous polo players can be traced back to the excellent quality of their ponies, without which they could never have reached the class they have, and the virtual monopoly in polo. Apart from the polo pony and the thoroughbred, only farm horses are bred and that in a rather haphazard manner, with little real selection or care.

I want right away to refute the common belief that South American success in the earliest horse shows after the war was mainly due to the fine quality of their horses. This is far from being true. In the Argentine horses are very inferior—at least as far as show horses are concerned. When I say inferior I mean inferior to the wonderful horses bred in France; the Anglo-Arabs, the Anglo-Normans, or the splendid Irish hunters and their English cousins and naturally far inferior to the great German horses, the Trakeneres, Hanoveraners and Holsteiners. I can truthfully say that a French or English horseman would feel he was disgracing himself by mounting even the best of South American show horses which, with very few exceptions, come from the farms where they have all been used for farm labour. Only the cavalry horses are remounts and some Thoroughbred horses coming from the race track are exceptions.

Chile also breeds her own horses but of a more wiry type, lighter in bone. This is explained by the fact that Chile is a very mountainous country, and in all such countries horses remain small and wiry although very strong. In contrast to the Argentinian horse, which has big flat feet like soup plates, the Chilean horse has rather small, very hard feet, like all horses from hilly districts. I noticed the same thing in California, where I was

From Pony-Light Horse

Great Britain—Mr. David Barker

From Pony-Light Horse

Italy—Signor Graciano Mancinelli

United States of America—Bill Steinkraus on Sindon

amazed by the small-sized shoes farriers usually carried with them.

The Mexican horse is very similar to the Chilean horse; on the small side, very wiry and fast, but more hot blooded. The only difference I have noticed is in the way they are saddled, and the different groups of muscles they therefore develop before even being trained to jump. The Chilean uses a very deep, short saddle, high in the cantle and bridge almost like an Arab saddle, thus giving his horse's hindquarters perfect freedom of movement. The Mexican saddles are too well known to need describing. I shall only mention that through their exaggerated weight and the fact that they are girthed too far back, the Mexican horses are inclined to use their hocks far more than other horses. The rider lets his weight slide back almost on the horse's kidneys, which tends to make the horse raise its head too much. The Mexicans therefore use their famous heavy bits with the high bridge, and even use large plates in the horse's mouth in order to counteract the effect of the rider's weight on the loins. Those bits look most cruel and horrifying to Europeans, but I have found that horses thus bitted have surprisingly soft mouths and react at the slightest pull of the reins.

When the Mexicans ride such horses later on in horse shows, with modern jumping saddles placed well to the front and using normal snaffle bits, they are forced to use short running martingales to keep their horses' heads down. The horse, relieved of the strong native bit, immediately throws its head too high for jumping events. I mention this only because many English friends have pointed this out to me whenever I condemned the martingale.

The United States breeds very fine riding horses. Nevada especially seems to produce a sturdy type of horse which is both heavier and stronger than the Mexican horse. The famous Morgan horses are too well known to need elaborating on, but there is one breed I want to mention: the so-called Palomino. Beige colour in a horse is always a throw-back, never a sign of quality. Whatever my American friends may think of their lovely

Palominos they are considered the worst horse by every Criollo, and if the Criollos know about anything they know about horses. There is a proverb in the Argentine which says: 'Unreliable like a beige horse', and a very true saying it certainly is. I have had many hundreds of horses in my life, of all colours and breeds, but I can confidently say that the beige horses are the worst, of whatever breed they may be. They are absolutely useless for any sort of equitation except for parades and spectacular displays, and this is what they are really being used for in the States. I admit a pretty Palomino is one of the loveliest sights any horse-man could wish to see, especially if the colour is slightly toasted and the horse has a platinum mane and tail. Palominos are superb, spirited and flashy—if one may use such an expression of a horse —but I have very seldom seen a Palomino winning a jumping event or doing even reasonably well in a dressage class. As riding hacks, especially for women, they are naturally unequalled. I can't imagine a lovelier sight than a pretty girl mounted western fashion on a Palomino, and I have never missed the opportunity of watching the famous rodeos and parades in California and Nevada.

The United States also produces one of the finest hunters in the world. I have passed whole days watching the judging of the hunter classes at the Madison Square Garden shows, always trying to find the first three myself but invariably failing. I could at the utmost eliminate two or three out of a class of twenty-five as inferior, but the rest were simply each one finer and more lovely than the other.

Another type of horse I have greatly admired is the American five-gaited horse, a remarkably beautiful animal, if good only for shows. The American three-gaited horse is only the American version of the English hack, but it is also very beautiful and well-proportioned.

But of all horse breeds I most admire the French horse. It seems to me that there is no horse in the world better suited to modern show jumping than the French Anglo-Arab and the

Anglo-Normand. For hunting there are better horses bred in England and Ireland, a little further away from the blood and thus more suited for rough work over uneven ground. I am a great admirer of the French school of equitation, which is one of the oldest and best in the world. If I now make a certain criticism it is made only in the spirit of fair sportsmanship; and perhaps it might also help the fine French horsemen even to better their remarkable records. French riders, in my opinion, ought to win ever single event they enter—because of the fantastic quality of their horses. If they fail to do so, as they have often done in the past, it is, in my belief, due only to the very inferior construction of the French saddle. French saddlers may not like this criticism, but I sincerely believe that if the construction of their saddles were improved French riders would be unbeatable. In the chapter dealing with saddles and gear I shall enlarge on this. Here I shall mention only the main defect of the French saddle known as the Danloux. It does not give sufficient support to the rider and acts exactly contrary to the English saddle. It throws the rider too far forward, practically on the horse's neck, thus interfering with the free movement of the horse.

Lately I have seen several German horses, the first to come out of that country after the war. They were splendid animals —big and powerful though less agile than the French horse and perhaps not as bold as the English horse and not as wise to difficult ground as the Irish horse. French riders and breeders were quite worried about the quality of these German horses and insisted that they would soon become very stiff competitors in the Continental shows, but I still believe that they will never be able to beat the Anglo-Arabs. In France, I have seen Anglo-Arabs standing easily up to 16.2 hands and weighing at least 1,100 to 1,200 lb., while the Argentinian-bred Anglo-Arabs hardly ever reached 15.3 and never weighed over 1,000 lb. The same apparently happened in Spain. I have seen many Hispano-Anglo-Arabs, as they are called. They all showed signs of inbreeding, were leggy, with almost flat withers and mules' backs. I was told that Spain had regularly to import fresh blood to keep the breed going at all. But there is one breed in Spain which is excellent— the Andalusian. This type originated from the Berber horses, and these horses therefore have a lot of Arab blood in them but are heavy and very sturdy. They are invariably bold and fiery horses; the only defect I find in them is the shortness and thickness of their necks, and narrow hindquarters which make them practically useless for show jumping.

Since this book was first written in 1953 a great number of changes have occurred in show jumping. The courses laid out in many instances, have become shorter and more tricky, to say the least. The combined obstacles, double and triple jumps are, indeed, sometimes laid out in such a way as to make it almost an acrobatic feat to get over them without faults, and speed is often the winning factor in such events. (I shall come back to that point in the later chapter on courses, etc.) Consequently horses must be faster and suppler to negotiate such artificially created handicaps and at the same time to race against the clock. They must be capable of negotiating very high obstacles at high speeds, and there is only one horse that can do that successfully—the Thorough- bred. For years I have naturally been giving the advice that only Thoroughbreds should be used in big jumping events if the competitors hope to win. I have always held that anything any crossbred horse can do a Thoroughbred horse can do faster and better, except perhaps pull beer wagons. The Thoroughbred, if trained with patience and not rushed, will become by far the best qualified horse for show jumping and will easily beat even the biggest show jumpers still used today, specially when a matter of speed decides the winner of an event.

In the last years I have noticed an ever increasing amount of Thoroughbreds being used in big shows, except perhaps in Puissance events, but even in those events the Thoroughbred will eventually beat every other horse. In earlier days they were too expensive for ordinary show jumping, but lately, with the prices paid today for first-class show jumpers the price of the

Thoroughbred has become quite acceptable. Recently I was present when 50,000 dollars were paid for a first-class jumper in Spain, a country in which riders are on the whole less well off than in other European countries. In Germany I was told, the same amount was paid for a Thoroughbred dressage horse.

The world record for High Jumping is today still held, after twenty-one years, by a Thoroughbred, Huaso, ridden by Captain Laragguibel of Chile, and the world's Broad Jump record is also held by a Thoroughbred, Amadao Mio, ridden by Lieutenant-Colonel Lopez de Hierro of Spain: this record has stood since 1951. So why shouldn't Thoroughbreds also win all the ordinary events, *if* they have been trained with patience, of course.

Although I have stated that courses, in many cases, are shorter and more tricky there has also been a very evident trend in recent years towards long galloping courses, often incorporating permanent obstacles. Outstanding examples of courses of this type are those at Hamburg, Aachen and at the Hickstead All-England arena, the latter presided over by Mr. Douglas Bunn.

At Rome, additionally, where leading competitions including the World Championship have been held, the course almost approaches the sort that would not be out of place in a cross-country event.

Chapter Two

Horse and Rider:
The Making of the Show Jumper

THE FIRST TRAINING LESSONS OF YOUNG HORSES

I have always been greatly interested in the question of the
early training of the young horse. I maintain that it is as important
as the correct education of children. I want to refute emphatically
the old-established belief that horses are born good or bad. There
is no animal in the world that I know of that shows a tendency
to be savage. True, every horse, like every man, has its own
personality more or less enhanced by its surroundings, and the
treatment it gets from man, but I maintain and can prove that
no horse is really born bad. It becomes so only after bad treatment.

With horses it is exactly the same thing as with youngsters.
If they are started early enough and treated intelligently they
become good horses, obedient to man and tolerant of him even
if they don't like him. There are naturally both strong and weak
characters among horses, as with children, but it is all only a
question of patience and comprehension on our part. If the teacher
is impatient and irritable his pupils won't learn much—they will
be confused and could hardly be blamed if their education is
somewhat lacking as a result. I, personally, have found hardly

any real difference between a boy of ten and a colt; they seem to react almost identically—impulsively and ever ready for mischief. It is up to us to coach them, control them and guide them. I have never blamed and punished a horse for its shortcomings, but always the man who broke it in and trained it, just as an intelligent man could hardly blame and punish a child for something it simply was not taught, but rather the teacher. Colts need to feel the hand of the teacher from time to time, just as youngsters do, but punishment should never be brutal; rather explanatory and then always at the very moment of misbehaviour. I have broken in many horses, or watched them being broken in, and have advised the man in charge. I can say confidently that the whole future of the horse depends on the treatment it gets when it comes for the first time in contact with man, the rider.

In England, horses are usually treated very gently as foals and when first handled and ridden, but I have also found that many English horses behave like spoiled brats. I have personally owned young racehorses which seemed to take a great pleasure in rearing and coming down on the shoulders of their grooms. Not trying to kill or even hurt—merely in a playful mood. But a horse weighs a lot and can easily injure a man. Every young horse needs to be taught respect for man. Respect it can get only if correctly treated—with kindness when good and with a little harshness when spiteful. Young colts are just as spiteful and mischievous as young boys and quite as nasty—if they can get away with it.

We must always bear in mind that neither young nor old horses love man. It is a popular fallacy that horses often love their masters—only dogs will do that and no other animal I know of. The horse just about 'tolerates' man, if trained correctly and broken in with patience. The horse truly loves only three things: to eat, to sleep and to roll happily on a dunghill after careful grooming! I have often listened to polo players insisting that their ponies 'love' to play and run after the ball; this just as silly as when show riders boast that their show-jumper 'loves' to jump. The polo pony will obey quickly the reflexes of his rider just as the jumper will try his best to help his rider over an obstacle, but it will never in its life love doing it. I will mention here an incident I witnessed in Australia before the war. A farmer who lived alone on a farm near Sydney, but pretty far away from other farms, went to town for some shopping. It was a hot day and from shopping he soon turned to drinking and went on quite a spree and from a spree into a drunken brawl, and he finally landed up with a badly injured head in the local hospital. When he was released from hospital after fifteen days with a stitched-up head he drove back to his farm to find that ten of the eleven horses he had left enclosed in a fenced-in paddock had died of thirst! Now that fence was only 4 ft. 6 in. high and the water tank only some ten feet away; thus only *one* of the eleven horses had the intelligence to leap over that rather low fence and get to the water. I mention this incident only to prove my point that horses loathe to jump. They will always avoid or by-pass any obstacle in their way if they can help it and only in most extreme cases will a horse jump. The horse has only three natural movements—walking, trotting and cantering; any others must be taught and taught with patience and common sense but *never* with brutality. It is as foolish to punish a young horse for having knocked into an obstacle as to beat a boy for making a mistake in his Latin grammer during his first lesson.

Be patient with your young horse, teach it to jump in such a way that the horse does not even realise that it is doing something unnatural, and *always* reward it even for the slightest effort. But never punish it for something you have not taught it properly. Young horses are like young boys, as I said, and liable to all sorts of pranks and mischief. We do not beat our youngsters for every mistake they make but try to reason with them; we try to make them understand that they have done something wrong. Only if every other means has proved useless would we punish a child corporally. The same goes for the young horse. I have myself broken in practically all the foals and fillies I breed, all of them

Thoroughbreds. Very seldom did I have to use the whip but I did use lots of sugar.

I have broken in those young horses from the halter to the girth and finally to the saddle and to the rider only with kindness, sugar and caresses. Only very rarely did I have to punish them and then only *immediately* after bad behaviour but never later out of temper. The horse thinks like a horse and not like a human being and it is no good trying to change its personality and natural instincts.

When training the young horse I very strongly advocate the same methods that I have explained in detail in the chapter on 'Alternative Method of Training' on page 82. These should be used, even if the horse is only two years old. If a young horse is of normal build the weight of the rider on its back is practically immaterial, only as long as the pace is *very slow,* and the ground very deep and soft. After a couple of months a foal or fillie will have developed strong enough muscles to take any rider's weight.

THE MODERN SEAT FOR SHOW JUMPING

This seat has been wrongly called the forward seat, the monkey seat and, more often, the Italian seat. None of these names is really correct—it was merely the excellent idea of a Yankee jockey by the name of Tod Sloan, and the true definition is really 'the balanced seat'. Funnily enough, few horsemen know this even in the States, where they usually refer to it as the forward or Italian seat, as in England and the Dominions.

England, when Tod Sloan landed there and won his first race, was the uncontested leader in the riding, breeding and training of horses. The conservative trainers and owners were vastly amused at his peculiar style and christened it the 'monkey seat'. They were not then aware that they had witnessed the most revolutionary thing in riding for the last two thousand years— since Alexander's Macedonian cavalry used shoes for the first time for their horses when crossing the Khyber Pass.

When Sloan went on winning one race after another, beating the best English jockeys on far better horses, they became thoughtful and finally came to the conclusion that he 'must have got something there'. As there is—and always has been—a lot of money involved in the breeding, training and racing of horses, the conservative British for once waived their instinctive dislike of anything foreign and sat down to study Sloan's methods. Being excellent horsemen themselves they soon found that the secret of Sloan's success lay in the fact that he kept his weight on the horse's withers and thus off the horse's loins. It was so simple that the British jockeys could have kicked themselves for not having thought of it. To safeguard the great financial interests vested in racing, the British were obliged to adopt this new fancy seat. Accordingly, when they afterwards rode on the Continent in that style the French, Germans and Italians quite naturally mistook it for a new British method, since they had always automatically taken their cue from England in anything connected with horses, and with good reason. On the Continent, therefore, this seat soon became known as the English Jockey Seat, and it made English jockeys so famous that even today Chantilly is almost a suburb of Newmarket.

Let us analyse Sloan's idea:

(1) We all know that the horse's engine is located in its hindquarters. Therefore, to allow that engine its maximum output, it must not be throttled—that is, the hindquarters must not be burdened with the rider's weight. They must be left free to move. Like all quadrupeds the horse uses its hindlegs for propulsion and its forelegs for steering and to allow its hindlegs to come forward for another stride.

(2) We also know that the horse's natural movements are three—walking, trotting and cantering. Jumping is not a natural movement, though most riders make the silly remark that their horses are 'natural jumpers'. A horse has far too much sense to jump if it can possibly avoid it; it will jump only if

forced by the rider to do so and when it cannot 'get away with' going round the jump. A good huntsman will never deliberately make his horse jump when he can avoid an obstacle without waste of time.

It is logical to assume, therefore, that if Tod Sloan's new seat is more effective than the old-fashioned hunting seat for getting a faster gallop out of the horse, it must also be better for jumping, a definitely unpleasant movement for the horse and executed only under compulsion.

It is possible that, had the prize money in ordinary show jumping been four thousand guineas instead of forty, the conservative British would soon have adopted the monkey seat for show jumping as well as for racing, or at least a modified version of it.

When the English jockeys started riding on the Continent in the new fashion they were naturally much admired since they beat the best Continental jockeys and riders hollow. Two Italian officers, endowed with observant minds and quick wits, studied their technique and started applying it in a modified way for cavalry training. Thus there developed in Tor di Quinto what is today called the modern seat or, erroneously, the forward, Italian or monkey seat.

Frederico Caprili and Piero Santini undoubtedly deserve praise for having originated modern cavalry training and for having fundamentally changed all the methods hitherto in use. All they really did, however, was to take an excellent American idea and modify it for application to all-round riding and cavalry training. Most countries in the world which were keen on horsemanship and all sports connected with it soon adopted these modern methods, with perhaps a few exceptions in some English-speaking countries. (Here I wish again to distinguish between civilian riders and cavalry officers, for every cavalry school throughout the world soon adopted the modern cavalry training methods as established in Italy, with some changes.) Among civilians, however, the modern method was spurned for many years as 'Dago trick-riding', and this is still the case in some countries after fifty years, incredible as it may seem. Show jumping has been completely revolutionised and courses have changed rapidly to become what they are today—elaborate and scientifically constructed events, calculated to improve the horse's performance, raise the standard of horsemanship and at the same time make show jumping safe.

The most important equestrian event at the Olympic Games is a concentration of Frederico Caprili's modern methods—that is, the three-day event, or, as we call it in South America, 'the combined Caprili'. This consists of (1) a cross-country, (2) an elementary dressage test, and (3) a show jumping event. Each of the three parts is as important as the other two. This is yet another proof of the importance of including elementary dressage in the basic training of every horse. I will try to give the reasons as briefly as possible:

A horse is not built to carry a man on its back, since no animals were created to be slaves to man. A horse's spine is strong enough to keep its long body together and also to take quite a lot of pressure, but immediately some 180 lb. is suddenly placed on it, it sags. The horse instinctively braces its whole body to support the unaccustomed weight, and in doing so it uses the muscles normally used to produce speed. It therefore cannot use its muscles as freely as it would without a weight on its back and consequently cannot give its best performance.

Elementary dressage is necessary, therefore, to help the horse gradually to develop those muscles which are necessary to support the rider's weight without handicapping its free movements. The horse can never develop these muscles in a couple of months, nor can it ever learn the correct flexion and acquire suppleness of neck and body in that time. The teaching of elementary dressage should be spread over a period of at least six to eight months and should be repeated at least once a week after the horse has gained its natural balance and learned the aids.

I observed earlier that the horse does not need to be a perfect *haute école* horse before starting to learn to jump but, like the rider, it must have basic elementary dressage training before being taught anything else.

Elementary dressage teaches the rider the following things:

(1) To place his weight on that part of the horse which is best suited for carrying weight—that is, as near as possible to the withers.

(2) To give the horse the necessary aids with as little obvious movement of the hands and legs as possible.

(3) To keep the horse *collected* (not to be confused with *gathered,* as this means flexion but never collection).

This book deals with modern show jumping, however, and not with elementary dressage. I take it for granted that no one in his senses will start jumping when he can hardly sit a horse correctly.

Many excellent books have already been written about the so-called 'forward seat'. All I shall do here is to explain its function and technique and why this 'balanced seat' is essential for modern show jumping.

Everyone knows that horses naturally dislike jumping, whatever individual riders may say. They have to be trained to it. Any cavalryman will tell you that a horse tends to avoid all forms of concentrated work, and really enjoys only three things —eating, drinking and rolling in the dust.

We also know what a horse needs to be a successful jumper:

(1) A free back with as little weight as possible on its loins.

(2) A free mouth so that it can stretch out its neck. This is essential for two reasons:

(a) For sizing up correctly the height and depth of the obstacle.

(*b*) For balancing its body. The horse's long neck
is its only means of balance—it must therefore be given
all the freedom possible. This is why it is so dangerous
to use a martingale—but I shall deal with that later.

(3) A certain amount of speed is essential to get the horse's
long body and hindlegs over a jump. The broader the
jump, the more speed required. If an athlete needs a
certain speed to jump over an obstacle with depth,
a horse needs at least three times that speed to clear
the same obstacle. I do not know what speed an athlete
would need to jump, shall we say, a double oxer 4 ft.
high by 6 ft. deep, but I know exactly what speed a horse
would require, and that is 400 yards a minute, at least.

The modern seat, therefore, is based on these two main factors:
(1) Freedom of neck and back through a correct seat and (2) The
necessary speed to clear obstacles.

For the modern seat the rider needs first of all a modern
saddle. The ordinary English saddle is, to put it mildly, absolutely
inadequate for correct modern show jumping. Only with a
modern saddle will the rider get the grip he needs to remain in
a correct position all the time and at the same time give the horse
the necessary aids and the freedom of the head which is absolutely
indispensable. I will explain the saddle question later on.

The modern seat is on exactly the same lines as Tod Sloan's
jockey seat, except that the stirrups are longer. They are, however,
sufficiently short to shorten the angles of the rider's thighs and
calves, in order to strengthen the grip. I will give the reader two
examples of the methods used in the army to explain to new
recruits the best grip on a horse:

(1) Take an oblong soap-box and sit on it as you see riders
    sitting in hack classes—that is, leaning slightly back-
    wards, with the legs well stretched forward, gripping
    only with the knees.

(2) Attach a rope to the box and then suddenly jerk the box

forward. You will observe that the man sitting as described will fall backwards, if he does not fall off altogether.

(3) Repeat the test, but this time make the man on the box sit correctly—that is, leaning forward at an angle of 45 degrees, his feet and calves well back at an angle of 40 degrees, and ask him to grip as best he can. You will find that when the box is jerked forward he will hardly change his position at all.

To test the strength of the knee grip I suggest using the following trial:

(1) Make two men sit opposite each other on chairs.
(2) Let one man sit with his legs stretched forward and the upper part of his body slightly inclined backwards.
(3) Let him, in this position, try to force together the knees of his opposite number. (It is understood that they have to be of about the same strength.) He will find that this feat is practically impossible.
(4) Now make the man change his position. Make him lean forward, lower his knees and slide his feet back as far as he can without falling off the chair. Let him try to force his opponent's knees together in this position and he will find that he has suddenly far more strength in his knees.

The reason for this is obvious. In the second position he has shortened his muscles and also the levers of his muscles.

I cannot think of a better way of demonstrating the enormous difference between the grip of the rider in the old-fashioned and the modern seat. In the old-fashioned way of sitting the rider's only real grip on the horse is the two small points of his knees. He is thus only pivoting and not gripping. The greater the length of adhesion of the rider's muscles to the saddle the stronger, naturally, will be the grip. If the rider keeps his feet parallel to the horse's body his calf muscles are hardly in contact with the saddle, at least not enough to give the rider real support. Thus, when the horse stops suddenly the rider will be forcibly thrown forward on the horse's neck, as his only real grip is the two points where the knees touch the saddle. When, on the other hand, the horse suddenly shoots forward the rider will fall backward on the saddle's cantle and thus add an increased pressure on the horse's lions, making it drop its hindlegs when in the act of jumping.

The modern seat has three strong grips—that is, if the saddle allows it, and most old-fashioned saddles don't. The first grip is with the inner-thigh muscles, the second with the knees and the last and the strongest grip—with the calf muscles. The calf grip keeps the rider in his seat even if the horse should stop suddenly or peck. It also prevents the rider from falling suddenly forward and being hit by the horse's head when it stumbles or pecks. I can prove this to the reader quite easily. Take off the saddle and ride your horse for a few rounds bareback in the paddock. Start off by trotting, then go into a canter and you will soon see with what parts of the leg you are gripping the horse. You will find to your surprise that you hardly even touch the horse with your knees but grip for dear life with the inner-thigh muscles and mostly with your calves. Surely it is logical to assume that the best grip without a saddle should also be the best grip with a saddle? The horse's body remains the same, but a bad saddle apparently changes the rider's position. True the rider's leg position is somewhat shortened by the stirrups, but the fact remains the same. A good jumping saddle must allow the rider to grip with those three parts—the inner-thigh muscles, the knee and calf muscles—which, incidentally, can't work efficiently if the foot is not turned out at a 45-degree angle from the horse's body.

To convince the reader of the all-importance of the correct grip on the horse, the reader should always check up on his leg and foot position. First let the reader sit on his horse in the in-correct way still so often taught today, i.e. gripping hard with the knees and with the feet parallel to the horse's body. In this completely faulty position the reader should try to stand up in his stirrups and remain standing while the horse trots or canters. He will immediately find out that he will never be able to do this and that he will fall forwards or backwards. The reason is simple: The rider in this position is not *gripping* by only *pivoting* on two small points of his knee. *Now* the rider should adopt the *correct* position and there is only *one* such correct leg and foot position, that is achieved as follows: *step firmly in his stirrups with the heel as much down as possible and the point of the foot sticking out at least to an angle of 45 degrees.* The rider will immediately discover that he has a very strong grip on the horse with his calfs. In this position the rider will be able to stand up easily with his arms outstretched and remain standing even at a quite fast canter. I cannot think of a better example to convince the reader of the best position and firmest seat.

Another fallacy is that one should not be comfortable in the saddle lest one feel inclined to slacken one's knee grip. This belief is almost too stupid to merit comment. Obviously the rider can't be *too* comfortable in his saddle, for the more comfortable he is, the more freedom his hands and the upper part of his body will have, and no horseman should dream of starting to jump without first acquiring that freedom.

First of all, then, get a correct modern saddle, or forward seat saddle as they are still called, and then proceed as follows:

(1) Shorten your stirrups until the irons hit you a little above the ankle-bone. Put the ball of the foot into the stirrup or the whole foot home (I personally advocate the South American method of placing the stirrup on the ball of the foot only as this gives more spring).

(2) Grip with your knees firmly in the hollow formed by knee-rolls under the saddle-flaps, then slide your buttocks back as far as you can without releasing your knee-grip from the hollows.

(3) Incline your upper body forward at an angle of 45 degrees.

(4) Put your feet back just beyond the girth, turn your toes out at an angle of 45 degrees and keep your heels down as much as you can. In this position you will find that you have:

(a) A very strong grip with your calves.

(b) That your buttocks are well off the saddle and that you are only sitting on the inside-thigh muscles.

Once you have achieved this position hold it and do not change it whatever happens—whether you are walking, trotting, galloping, riding up or down the steepest slopes or approaching an obstacle, clearing it and continuing to the next obstacle. It is unnecessary to change your position because you are already firmly seated and perfectly balanced to take a jump. Do not, however, try to use the forward seat position on your old-fashioned saddle, or without having first learned to ride in the forward seat, since it is necessary to develop an entirely new set of muscles which are not used in the old-fashioned way of riding.

This, in a nutshell, is the whole theory of modern show jumping:

(1) Remember that you are only a passenger, so be as little of a burden as possible.

(2) It is the horse that is jumping, not you, so let it jump freely at the speed it requires.

(3) Let the horse decide when it has to take its forelegs off the ground and jump. Never try to show it when to jump—the horse knows better than you do.

All you can do is sit firmly, give the horse its head, keep your weight off its loins and give a strong pressure with your calves and heels when approaching a jump to increase the horse's speed. Anything else you may do will only handicap your horse's movements and make jumping even more difficult than it actually is. Sit still, therefore, and forget any acrobatics you may have been taught to 'make jumping easier for the horse', such as trying to slow down the horse, standing up in the stirrups, leaning forward on the horse's neck, etc. These movements have absolutely nothing to do with riding and are merely the logical consequence of the wrong seat in which you entered the ring and approached the jump, and use of the wrong saddle.

The nearer to the jump you get the more pressure you must exert on the horse with your legs in order to increase its speed. The more determination you show, the better your horse will jump. Every horseman knows that his mount feels the rider's nervousness instinctively and loses confidence. You must therefore give your horse all possible confidence by having first of all confidence in yourself.

I shall now try to analyse the acrobatic and highly intricate feats that an old-fashioned rider usually performs in a show ring.

(1) He comes in at a walk. When he gets near the starting flag he usually kicks his horse violently, chiefly to give himself courage and to prove to the poor animal that he is not afraid.

(2) When the horse, as a consequence of such treatment, breaks into a gallop, he jerks it back by sawing at its mouth and reduces its speed to a minimum.

(3) The nearer he gets to the jump, the more he slows down his horse, in order to 'place it correctly into the jump'. (I shall enlarge on this senseless endeavour later.)

(4) When the rider considers that it is time the horse got its forelegs off the ground he at length gets his buttocks off the saddle and suddenly throws his whole weight on the horse's neck. (This is called by riding masters 'rising in the stirrups and making it possible for the horse to jump', which is another proof that the hunting seat is not suitable for jumping.)

The rider naturally thinks that by leaning forward over the horse's neck he is making it easier for the horse to jump, but what he actually does is this: he suddenly throws an extra 40 to 70 lb. on the horse's forehand just when the poor animal is trying to get off the ground, having resigned itself to the weight

on its suffering loins and having decided to jump *malgré tout*!
The rider is forced to do this for the following reasons:

(1) Because his seat was wrong to start with, he feels that he must correct it by these acrobatic feats.

(2) Because the saddle he is using is absolutely useless for real jumping and does not give the rider the comfort that it should.

(3) Because no rider could possibly jump if he remained seated in the old-fashioned hunting seat as when he entered the ring, and this is because no human being has sufficiently strong stomach muscles to keep the upper part of his body in that position when the horse suddenly jerks its legs forward in the act of jumping.

The reader will know by experience what usually happens in such cases:

(1) The horse may refuse to jump at all under such coercion, with the rider sitting on it like a sack of potatoes.

(2) It may break out, if it still has a chance to do so.

(3) It will put in an extra short stride, to get the unaccustomed weight off its neck and forelegs and on to its loins again.

The last is what usually happens. The result is that when the horse finally jumps, the rider, who has already risen in his stirrups, thinking he has calculated the take-off just right and shown his horse when to jump, now falls violently forward, since the only points of contact he has with his horse are his knees. The horse, which is now too near to the jump, must literally jump with all four feet in the air and do what is called a 'cat jump'. The rider is then 'left behind', as it is called in horse language. He first falls forward, then back jabbing the horse's mouth, then falls forward again on his horse's neck when the animal lands on the other side. He will then hang on to his horse's neck for dear life and perform a series of acrobatic frog leaps in reverse, trying to get his buttocks back into the saddle again. If he succeeds he will probably be rewarded by a round of applause from the public, who invariably enjoy these acrobatic performances.

So far, so good. If, however, the jump happens to be an oxer with a depth of five to six feet the performance becomes even more painful. The unfortunate horse, whose speed has been reduced to a mere prancing, is now supposed to leap like a kangaroo over a six-foot-wide jump. Held back as it is, it may get its forelegs over the poles but will inevitably crash into the bars with its hind legs. And so on to the next jump. I need not continue describing this sad performance; the reader will no doubt have witnessed it many times at horse shows and may even have experienced it himself.

I could never understand what riding masters meant when they explained their pupils' mistakes to them and said that the rider was not 'with' his horse, was 'with' his horse, or was 'behind' his horse, when all the time he was sitting on it! The rider is forced to concentrate all his wits on the all-important matter of deciding exactly when the horse is going to jump, so that he can rise with it. He therefore has not time left to jump correctly, which is the reason he went into the ring for.

The modern seat has altogether eliminated placing, with all its attendant contortions. The rider is taught to let the horse do its own placing, but the horse has already been correctly placed by the men who laid out the course. Incidentally, it is useless to try to make a horse see things as we do because its eyes focus quite differently; it is therefore much better left alone.

It is extremely difficult to make a rider who has been trained in the old-fashioned way drop this habit of placing. I have noticed that riders who have already done some jumping before they started learning the modern seat will adapt themselves rapidly to the new method but will invariably revert to their bad habits and slow their horses down when approaching an obstacle, instead of increasing their speed. I used to insist on them closing their eyes and digging in their heels. If their seat was any good they kept it; if they had lapsed into bad habits and straightened up they were sadly left behind. This was the only way to make them check up on their seats. Hopeless cases I simply put back into the manège and started them off blindfold over low jumps, like beginners.

Every horseman who has jumped for some time knows that the slower the horse's speed the more difficult it is for the rider to maintain a proper seat over a jump. If the horse is practically at a standstill it is almost impossible to get over.

This book is written for the average rider who still has a great deal to learn, and all the advice given is naturally intended for him and not for the famous international horsemen. Experienced show riders like Colonels Llewellyn and Dudgeon, and Mr. White, have not to bother about placing their horses, although the onlooker may sometimes get the impression that they do. They simply feel every stride of their horse and can judge the speed at which it is approaching the obstacle by the cadence of the canter, and know when the horse is going to take off. To those riders the cadence of their mount's strides have almost become their own. They can measure them, stretch them and shorten them at will, exactly as any athlete can do with his own strides. If asked how they place their horse, they will say they simply know instinctively when their horse is going to take off and jump. But those are experienced horsemen; they have been riding for many years and have developed almost a sixth sense.

This is not the case with the average rider, certainly not with the novice rider. If a nervous rider has to count his horse's strides, work out accurately when it is going to jump, and so on, and at the same time has trouble with his seat, he is bound to make mistakes, misjudge the horse's speed and instead of helping it will impede its movements when trying to place it into the jump.

There is no sense in trying to teach a horse what the rider himself does not know. The best thing is to ride, ride boldly and with decision, give the horse encouragement and the necessary speed to get over the obstacle and not bother about when or how the horse is going to do it. Remember, horses have horse-sense and four strong legs of their own. They will know best how to do it, and must not be unnecessarily handicapped by the rider.

THE TRAINING OF THE MODERN SHOW RIDER

I have already mentioned that I take it for granted that a show rider is a *rider*, that is, that he has learned how to ride correctly before attempting to learn to jump. The following exercises are only for jumping; they are not elementary riding lessons.

I have also mentioned that I have experienced the greatest difficulty in training riders to jump who have previously jumped in the old-fashioned hunting seat. Such riders appeared to be fascinated by the oncoming jump: the nearer they got to it, the more they slowed down their horses and the more nervous they became, thereby communicating their nervousness to their horses. My advice to such riders is—never look at the first jump, but always at the last jump in a number of jumps. Give as much leg pressure as you can in front of every jump and look ahead.

In the chapter dealing with modern courses the reader will see that such courses are becoming more compact every day, and the close placing of the jumps leaves a nervous rider very little time to rectify an initial mistake such as loss of speed. He therefore cannot afford to bother about placing his horse, and in any case the men who laid out the course have already done that for him, far more accurately than he could do it himself. All he has to do is keep a cool head and ride strongly, giving his horse all the freedom it needs.

I don't want to write a purely technical book as so many excellent ones have already been written. All I shall do, therefore, is to give the reader the exercises that he simply *must* master before starting to jump, and the proper jumping training.

The first essential is the manège. Without a closed manège no one can possibly learn to jump. (This must not be confused with the special manège used exclusively for dressage classes.) The ideal manège is completely enclosed. The horse should not be able to see out, so that it will keep its mind on its work. The walls may be made of split poles, planks, bricks or even corrugated iron painted white, and should be about 7 ft. high and slightly inclined outwards. The floor should be as soft as possible; one foot thickness of wood shavings or sawdust is ideal.

It is never advisable to try to learn anything by yourself. There must always be a second person present who at least knows as much as you do, if you have not got an instructor, for he can see the mistakes you make and can help in the event of an accident.

We will now start with the different simplified exercises:

No. 1. Enter the manège, close the gate, and start walking round with loose reins.

No. 2. Take the reins in your right hand and start making large circles with the left arm. Keep this up for several rounds.

No. 3. Stretch out your left arm horizontally with the palm of your hand upwards. Now start turning your body from the waist upwards, first to the left and then to the right, holding your left arm up at shoulder height all the time. You must turn the whole upper body and not only the arm. Do this for several rounds.

No. 4. Execute three energetic stabbing movements with your left arm in quick succession—one forward, the second sideways and the third backward—by turning round as much as you can in the saddle without releasing your knees from their place. Keep this up also for several rounds.

No. 5. Change direction now and take the reins in your left hand.

No. 6. Start all over again, making the movements with your right hand. Each movement—three rounds.

No. 7. Execute all the above movements with one foot out of the stirrup.

No. 8. Execute all the above movements with both feet out of the stirrups—first, all the movements with one hand and then with the other.

The Duchess of Valencia: the importance of the calf grip, which allows absolute independence of the upper body and hands, is clearly shown in this picture.

Photo by Sosa, Mexico City. By courtesy of Mexican Embassy, London

Captain Ruben Uriza Castro, Mexican Cavalry

E. Wertheimer

A young horsewoman trained in another country by the author. Note perfect similarity in the position of the two riders and equal freedom of horses' movements

E. Wertheimer

Forward inclination of 45°, firm thigh-grip, knee well fitted into supports. Toes up and foot turned out at 45° give strong calf-grip. The hands are low and away from horse's neck

"Cape Times", Cape Town

A perfect example of the modern seat. Firm calf-grip gives freedom of hands and upper body

Great Britain—Mr. David Broome on Mister Softee

No. 9. Start from the beginning again with both feet in the stirrups but this time in a collected trot (that is, no posting).

No. 10. Repeat all the exercises in an extended trot (posting).

No. 11. Repeat all the exercises in a canter on both leads. When the pupil has mastered all these movements in a walk, trot and canter on both leads, he starts again right from the beginning.

No. 12. Back to a walk, with both feet in the stirrups but both arms doing the movements, with the reins tied in a knot and lying on the horse's neck.

No. 13. The same exercises as before, first with one foot out of the stirrup and then the other, in a walk, trot and canter.

We come now to a different group of movements:[1]

(1) Walk round with both feet in the stirrups but with the reins on the horse's neck. Then lean down to the left with both hands over your head, until you can touch your left foot, then your right foot.

(2) Put your hands on your hips and lean backward until you are lying on the horse's loins—then sit up again. Repeat this several times.

(3) The same thing all over again, but when you sit up bend over to the left and touch your foot; lie back again and then sit up and touch your right foot.

(4) Repeat all these movements in a walk, trot and canter.

(5) Start all over again, first with the left leg than with the right out of the stirrup, then with both feet out of the stirrups, in a walk, trot and canter.

It must be remembered that these exercises, though they form no part of jumping or of jumping lessons, are absolutely essential in order to form the basis of jumping—that is, the all-important independence of the upper part of the body from the horse.

We come now to the last movements, which are the most difficult:

(6) Standing still, drop your reins. Then throw your right leg over the horse's neck and sit with both legs on the near side (not, however, as in side-saddle).

(7) Throw your left leg over the horse's croup and sit facing the horse's tail.

(8) Throw the right leg over and sit with both legs on the off side.

(9) Throw the left leg over the horse's withers and sit normally again.

(10) Repeat the above in a walk.

(11) Repeat the above in a trot.

(12) Repeat the above in a canter. Now change direction and repeat the whole exercise in a clockwise direction.

Please note that in no circumstances must all this be done in one day; it should be spread over several months. The longer you take, the surer will you feel. You will do the last exercise better and will gain a better balance. I need not emphasise the supreme importance of balance in riding in general and jumping in particular.

Once the rider has mastered all these movements he will have acquired a pretty secure seat and an excellent balance, and can now start walking, trotting and cantering without reins. The best thing to do in a closed manège is let the horse do what it likes and go where it pleases. Keep your arms over your head, behind your back or put your hands on your hips. Finally, trot or canter with your hands in your pockets, or whilst you are lighting a cigarette. This is to check up on how firm and independent your seat has become through the exercises. The exercises should then be repeated bareback.

From my own experience I have found that most riders master all these exercises in a few months—some sooner, some later. They are as essential to a show jumper as shadow boxing and long cross-country runs are to the boxer. When I was training South American teams for great international events I made them go through these exercises for half an hour every day, to keep them in trim. A pupil who cannot do all these exercises has no business to start real jumping lessons, and has still less right to be in a jumping event. The training may take some time, but it is worth it to gain perfect balance and a good seat. There is no sport or prize in the world worth the pain and expense of a broken arm, leg, or neck. Riding should be a safe and pleasant sport, not a struggle to the death between horse and rider. These exercises are part of the daily routine in every cavalry school in the world, and they should certainly know what they are doing.

We now come to the real jumping lessons:

(1) Get in the jumping seat, as already explained.

(2) Place a single low jump, not higher than 2 ft. 6 in. by 3 ft. Start trotting round the manège in the forward seat, with the reins perfectly loose on the horse's neck. Hold your hands at least one foot lower than the horse's withers and 7 in. away from the horse's neck, with your elbows slightly bent, so that your lower arm forms with the reins a straight line to the horse's mouth. In this position approach the low jump without looking at it, and trot over it without touching the reins. The pupil must be made to throw his hands forward every time when jumping, exaggerating the movement.

(3) Carry on with this exercise for at least a dozen rounds. The man on the ground must watch that the rider does not look at the jump and does not try to interfere with the horse's movements. He must only hold his horse in, in case it breaks into a canter.

(4) Now place another jump on the other side of the manège. This time it must be a vertical jump—picket fence, single pole, low wall, or even a low brush, but not

higher than 2 ft. 6 in., and the pupil must take the two jumps a dozen times. The man on the ground must again watch that the rider does not slow down the horse and particularly that he throws his hands well forward the moment the horse jumps, the reins hanging loose all the time. If the pupil has done this properly without once losing his seat and falling backward he should stop jumping for that day.

(5) The next day the pupil must start all over again with the jumping exercises mentioned earlier, then two jumps are again placed in the manège and he starts trotting over them as on the previous day.

(6) When the onlooker is satisfied that the rider is going over the jumps without losing his seat the structure of the jumps should be changed to a low triple bar, low oxer, parallel bars or hog's back, and the height raised by 4 in.

(7) The rider does six or eight rounds, then takes both feet out of the stirrups and jumps thus for another ten rounds, all the time without holding the reins.

(8) The next day the rider, having done jumping exercises for half an hour, starts all over again with the jumping— first with the stirrups, then without them, then with one foot only in the stirrup. This is more difficult than jumping with both feet out of the stirrups.

(9) The next day, after the usual exercises, the rider must jump with the stirrups, then without them, then with one foot in the stirrup, and then take off the saddle and jump bareback.

(10) Jumping exercises again, then a few rounds over the two jumps at 2 ft. 8 in. The jumps must now be raised to 3 ft. and the rider must start again from the beginning, with and without the stirrups.

Jumping must be continued on these lines until, after a couple of months, the rider has reached 3 ft. 8 in. and does not lose his seat.

We come now to the second phase of the jumping training—
the gallop jump. At a height of 3 ft. 8 in. most horses will put
in one or two gallop strides before taking off; this another step
forward to the real gallop jump.

(1) Put up one single jump—3 ft. 4 in. high by 3 ft. deep—
then place one low jump, a cavalette (see fig. 1), exactly
35 feet in front of the real jump. (This first jump is not
a real jump but only an 18 in. 'placing jump'.) I will now
explain how the horse is placed in modern jumping.
When the rider comes at a good trot into the placing
jump he will see that the horse does not carry on again
in a trot after the jump but makes two gallop strides
and jumps over the real jump. Thus the horse is automatically placed at the correct distance for the jump—
*not, however, by slowing it down in the old-fashioned way but
by increasing its speed from a trot to a gallop.*
The rider will soon see how it is done in the training
of the horse.

(2) The rider starts all over again with jumping exercises. As
these must be executed every time before starting to
jump, I shall not mention them any more, taking it for
granted that the rider does them. They serve to warm
up the horse and limber up the rider before starting to
jump. The rider now goes over this jump a dozen times,
always coming in at a trot and letting his horse gallop
freely only between the placing jump and the real jump.
Once over the jump, he brings the horse back, into a trot.

(3) Another jump is now placed on the other side of the
manège and a placing jump put 22 ft. in front of it. This
distance allows the horse only one stride and jump, but
will place the horse quite as accurately as the previous
35 ft. (see fig. 2).

(4) Exercises again, then jumping over the two jumps, the
rider always brings the horse back to a trot after clearing

the jump. (By 'jump', incidentally, I mean the real jump, not the placing one.)

(5) The same routine—both feet out of the stirrups, then one foot and finally bareback.

(6) The jumps may now be raised to 4 ft. as it doesn't make the slightest difference if the jumps are 4 in. higher, providing the horse is correctly placed and has the correct speed.

(7) The distances between the placing jumps and the real jumps must now be altered—the first distance being reduced to 22 ft. and the second lengthened to 35 ft. The next day change them again, until the rider is no longer thrown off-balance by the change of distances.

(8) Now place another jump 22 ft. away from the first one. The rider will then come in at a trot over the placing jump, make two gallop strides up to the first jump, clear it, land, make one more gallop stride and jump over the second jump. This is the first form of a combined obstacle which forms the basis of modern show courses.

(9) Keep changing the distances, but always measure them from the placing jump to the centre of the first jump and from the centre of the first jump to the centre of the second jump. Both these jumps should be spread jumps. This is of the utmost importance, otherwise your distances will be wrong. Therefore never measure jumps from and to the nearest pole but always from centre to centre.

(10) When the pupil is able to keep his seat well over two such groups of jumps bareback, the third phase of his training begins.

The rider is now ready for the real gallop jump.

(1) After the usual exercises he starts off in a canter with loose reins, goes over the placing jump in a canter and continues thus all round for a dozen rounds. First with both feet in the stirrups, then out, then one out, and finally bareback.

(2) The procedure is more or less the same the next day—exercises and then canter jumps, but the jumps may be raised to 4 ft. and must be varied continually.

(3) The same thing all over again, but the rider now keeps one arm behind his back, then the other, and finally both arms behind his back.

(4) Both arms should now be held straight up in the air over the rider's head, then stretched out horizontally sideways at shoulder height. Finally both hands should be put in the pockets. All this time, of course, the procedure previously described should be carried out.

Now to the third phase—the gallop jump without placing jump. Only after the pupil has mastered all these exercises, and can jump without holding the reins, has he practically achieved the all-important independence of the upper body and has a firm seat. From now on exercises must be started with reins but without real contact with the horse's mouth. Gradually the length of rein must be shortened until the pupil has learned to give his horse absolute freedom of mouth, and contact is established. The teacher must pay special attention to this fact and the pupil's horse must always jump with maximum freedom. Should the pupil sometimes make a mistake, and jerk the horse's mouth, jumping without reins should be started all over again and later on repeated from time to time.

(1) Remove all the jumps except one. Lower this to about 3 ft., start off in a canter, approach the jump in a canter and let the horse jump freely, without interfering in the least with its paces.

(2) Now blindfold the rider and let him start off in the straight leading up to the single jump. If he has a firm seat he will go over the jump without even moving in the saddle. If he is not afraid, let him continue blindfolded round the paddock and thus jump a full round.

(3) Remove the bandage and start all over again with the

previous exercises, with and without stirrups, bare-back, and finally without holding the reins, when a few lengths away from the obstacle.

After a couple of months the rider will be able to do all this easily and can then start on the next stage—the jumping lane. A jumping lane should be fenced in on both sides by 7 ft. railings and should be 14 ft. wide. In this lane place anything from 10 to 25 jumps of varying heights and varying structures and depths, but always at correctly measured distances. I will give the distances here, though they really belong to the chapter on show courses:

(1) One stride and jump—minimum distance, 22 ft.
maximum distance, 27 ft.
(2) Two strides and jump—minimum distance, 35 ft.
maximum distance, 40 ft.
(3) Three strides and jump—minimum distance, 48 ft.
maximum distance, 53 ft.

These distances are quite sufficient for the jumping lane, where obstacles should never be more than three strides apart.

Obstacles in the jumping lane should at first be only cavalettes —that is, two crosses connected by a pole. They can be made of varying heights simply by making the crosses irregular by not fixing the two arms in the centre. This will automatically give three different heights for each cavalette.

(1) Place as many as fifteen or twenty cavalettes in the jumping lane.

(2) Vary the distances between them by anything from 9 to 50 ft. The distance of 9 to 14 ft. is never applied in a show course because it does not allow the horse a stride between two jumps. This distance forces the horse to 'bounce' between the two cavalettes. It is, however, always used for training both horse and rider as it gives the horse elasticity, builds up its hindquarters, and teaches the rider to keep a firm seat.

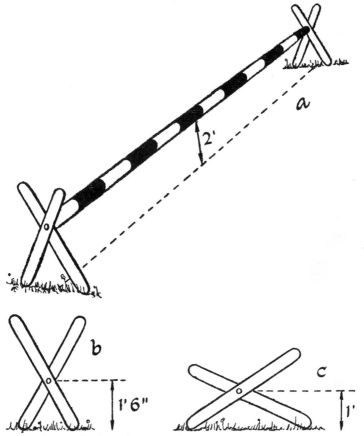

Fig. 1.—*Cavalette:* SHOWING CONSTRUCTION TO GIVE THREE
DIFFERENT HEIGHTS:

(a) On longer arms of cross: 2 ft. high.
(b) On shorter arms of cross: 1 ft. 6 in. high.
(c) On flat sides of cross: 1 ft. high.

(3) The cavalettes could be disposed thus:

1 to 2	25 ft.
2 to 3	22 ft.
3 to 4	10 ft.
4 to 5	9 ft.
5 to 6	9 ft.

6 to 7	11 ft. (thus forcing the horse to stretch a little more)
7 to 8	22 ft.
8 to 9	11 ft.
9 to 10	22 ft.
10 to 11	10 ft.
11 to 12	35 ft.

and so on, as long as your lane allows.

(4) The pupil now starts in a canter through the lane; first with reins and both feet in the stirrups, then with both feet out of the stirrups, then one foot out, then with one arm in the air or behind his back, then with both hands off the reins, in the air, horizontally sideways, or in his pockets. Finally bareback and without holding the reins.

These exercises should not be rushed or the rider may fall off and lose his nerve. Since the horse will go much faster when he drops the reins, the man on the ground should first of all measure the distances between the jumps and change them from the minimum to the maximum, as tabled, to allow for the increase in speed.

The exercises should be spread over a period of at least two weeks, although some riders may find that they can do them all the very first day. This, however, is unlikely. Moreover, it must not be assumed that the rider is then qualified to go straight away into the jumping paddock and over courses. These exercises are the daily training for jumping fitness. There is no point in learning them and then forgetting all about them. You might just as well learn to write and then never use a pen again. The exercises must be repeated at regular intervals, even if the pupil has already entered in several novice events.

(5) The cavalettes should now be replaced with ordinary low jumps—picket fences, walls, post and rails, oxers (not too deep—about 3 ft. 6 in.), hogs' backs, etc., and the pupil should then follow the same procedure as in Exercise 4.

(6) Fit in several cavalettes between the jumps, where you want the rider to take no strides between the jumps.

(7) Raise the heights and increase the depths of the obstacles gradually, but never go over 3 ft. 8 in. as this is quite sufficient for a jumping lane.

We come now to the last phase—jumping over a proper course in the jumping paddocks. Before the pupil is allowed in there, however, he must pass his test in the jumping lane, to see how firm his seat has become.

Let him enter the lane in a canter. When he reaches the first jump in the lane he must drop the reins, take out a box of cigarettes and matches, and emerge from the lane with a lighted cigarette in his mouth.

Let him then do it all over again with his hands in his pockets. Only if he can do this is he ready for the next step—jumping over a course in an open paddock.

Put up a low course, not higher than 3 ft. 4 in. with spread jumps of a maximum spread of 4 ft. The pupil is now in the open field and for the first time on his own. He should know by now how short or long to hold his horse, but must still take correction from the man on the ground. He must have some contact with his horse's mouth, but not too strong, and must give the horse all the freedom of mouth it requires one stride before the jump. The instructor must tell him every time whether he gave the horse enough freedom or held it too short. If the pupil is going too slowly the instructor should shout 'More legs!' If too quickly, he should shout 'Checking!'

When the pupil is out of a straight line of jumps and is negotiating a corner to approach the next line of obstacles he should hold the reins shorter in a firmer grip, relaxing his hold when out of the bend.

When the pupil has jumped twice a week for a month or so over such varied low courses he must return to the manège for the last stage of his training; that is, the use of the legs. I have already mentioned that leg pressure is absolutely essential in later show jumping, when the jumps are high and deep. I will now give the necessary exercises for gaining this all-important leg pressure.

(1) Build up a 4 ft. triple bar and put a cavalette (placing jump) 35 ft. in front of it.

(2) Let the pupil start off in a trot round the manège; trot over the placing jump; then give the horse pressure with his legs and clear the jump after two gallop strides. This must be repeated many times, after half an hour of the usual jumping exercises.

(3) Increase the distance between the placing jump and the real jump from 35 ft. to 37 ft. and let the pupil again start off in a trot and go slowly over the placing jump. He will find that he will have to give greater leg pressure to get his horse over the jump in two strides. If his leg pressure is not strong enough the horse will put in an extra stride for lack of speed. This proves whether the rider has used his legs or not.

(4) The distance can now be stretched to a maximum of 40 ft. The reader will now realise what great leg pressure the rider must develop to get his horse over in two strides, since this distance corresponds in an open jumping event to a speed of 550 yards per minute.

(5) The distance between the placing jump and the jump must now be changed from two strides to one stride. First of all, reduce the distance to 22 ft. and let the pupil start off again in a slow trot over the placing jump, then give the horse leg pressure and make it clear the jump with one stride and jump.

(6) Increase the distance gradually from 22 ft. to the maximum 27 ft. and see that the pupil really does use his legs.

When the rider has done this for a month, and has proved that he knows how to use his legs, he is almost ready for a novice event.

The reader will at this stage find that the only great difference between the training of horse and rider will now appear. A novice rider who only needs to jump over courses of a maximum height of 3 ft. 6 in. must be trained to get over jumps of 4 ft. 6 in. in the closed manège with and without stirrups, saddle and reins. The horse, on the other hand, should never be asked to jump higher than the jumps in its own category. It must learn to negotiate higher jumps gradually by jumping in novice courses many times. Having thus developed the necessary muscles, it will automatically learn how to make a slight effort and get over a jump six inches higher.

A novice should always train on a good horse, especially when it comes to jumping over courses and later over higher jumps in the manège. The training for this is as follows:

(1) Place a 4 ft. 4 in. jump in the manège with a cavalette 35 ft. away from it and start all over again, with and without stirrups, saddle and reins.

(2) Change the structure of the jump and increase its height gradually until 4 ft. 8 in. is reached, continuing with the exercises as above.

(3) Lower the height of the jump to four feet and remove the placing jump. The pupil starts off in a canter and jumps over, giving the horse the correct freedom of mouth, but he must gather the reins and re-establish contact with the horse the instant it lands, and keep this contact until he reaches the jump again.

(4) Raise the height of the jump gradually until it again reaches 4 ft. 8 in. and practise jumping over it as in Exercise 1.

The pupil should now be taken out again to the jumping paddock. Lay out a course of about sixteen jumps, with a couple of jumps 4 ft. high and with a slightly wider spread than in ordinary novice events.

The pupil must practise over this higher course for a month or so, but should still have someone on the ground to help him to control the speed, and to point out such mistakes as not enough or too much contact with the horse's mouth, not allowing the horse enough freedom of mouth during jumping, too little leg pressure. Only when a rider can confidently negotiate such courses as these is he ready to participate in a novice event—never earlier. As I have said before, a show ring is a place where you show the public what you have learned; it is not a place where you learn jumping. Therefore do your training at home or in a competent riding school and gain experience in riding clubs or in friends' paddocks, but do not try to gain experience in a show ring. You will only make a fool of yourself and will lose confidence.

If you learn to jump in the manner set out above (which is the usual cavalry training for officers who are going in for show jumping) you will gain an excellent seat, a steady nerve and, most important of all, you will eliminate the factor of danger, which has no place in real sport, even if it undoubtedly adds spice to such spectacles as bull-fights. A future show rider must learn slowly and gradually. Only by riding and jumping and yet more jumping can a rider ever hope to perfect his style and eventually reach the international class. Hence the deliberately slow, thorough training used in all modern schools. The result of this slow and gradual training is that the rider ultimately feels as much at ease in the saddle as in an armchair, and a correct seat will have become second nature to him.

I should like to mention here that I doubt very much if anyone can really learn to ride from books. Every novice needs constant supervision by someone who knows what he is talking about. In fact, I have only once met someone who succeeded in learning to ride from books, and this was a girl of seventeen, Heather Carruthers, whom I watched jumping in various shows in one of the British Dominions and who amazed me by the perfection of her style and position. She sat in a perfect modern seat, used her legs and hands correctly, and succeeded in winning most of the events. Moreover, she never placed her horse and was streets ahead of all the other riders, most of whom rode extremely badly. Naturally, I was interested and made enquiries about her. She told me that her father had been her only teacher and he, having had only a short cavalry training himself, had taught his daughter with the aid of books. He specially recommended Lieutenant-Colonel Chamberlin's book on Fort Riley methods as the one which had been most helpful. I congratulated him on his success and assured him that, given the right horse, his daughter was capable of winning an international event anywhere. At that time she had already won 250 prizes, and when her father later sent her to Ireland to perfect her training under the expert guidance of Colonel Dudgeon in Dublin I heard with pleasure that she won three important open events in Ireland after a stay of only three weeks.

This is, however, an exceptional case and was made possible only by the girl's enthusiasm and by the great interest her father took in her training. If this girl keeps on jumping she will soon be heard of in the great international events. I knew one other girl—a South American—who rose from the third category to the first, but although her father bought her the best horses in the country she was unable to win in the top category in the Argentine, which is a stiffer course than that laid out for the *Prix des Nations* at the Olympic Games and is run at 500 yards a minute.

It has been my experience that although women usually learn the modern seat far more easily than men, and make far better riders in the intermediate categories, they seem to lose their nerve when it comes to really big jumps of thirty in a course. I know of only a few who have reached international class: Señorita Valdez of Mexico; Señorita Zulof of Argentina; Mademoiselle Cancre of France; Miss Iris Kellet of Ireland; Miss Pat Smythe and Miss Mary Whitehead of England. I sincerely hope that one of these girls will one day prove that modern women really are equal to men—as they so often tell us!

THE TRAINING OF THE HORSE FOR SHOW JUMPING

As in the case of the show rider, I take it for granted that a horse destined for jumping has been properly schooled in elementary dressage. Only when it has learned to walk, trot and canter correctly with the weight of a rider on its back should it be allowed to start jumping. The training in elementary dressage, which takes anything up to six months or a year, enables the horse to develop the muscles which are necessary to counteract the effect of the rider's weight on its back and is NOT *haute école!* I shall now give a short explanation of what *haute école,* or dressage, really is.

Dressage originated thousands of years ago in Arabia, the home of the Thoroughbred. The Arabs, expert horsemen as they were, noticed the effect of the rider's weight on the horse's back and devised methods to correct this. They trained their horses to develop muscles which they had not used before being saddled and gradually developed aids which made the horse under a rider perform precisely the same graceful movements as those of a young, unsaddled colt. Thus *haute école* is not, as old-fashioned riding masters would tell you, 'artificial circus work' but simply the perfection of training and the result of long and patient schooling by expert horsemen.

The Arabs took their training methods over to Spain when they conquered that country in the eighth century under the Amir Al Tarrik (hence, incidentally, the name of Gibraltar—the Djebel Al Tarrik—the hill where Tarrik crossed over to Europe). Spain remained under Arab domination for over seven hundred years and the Arabs bred and trained fine horses there. During the reign of Don Carlos, later the Emperor Charles V of Germany, these famous Spanish horses began to become known on the Continent. Two Andalusian horses, trained in dressage in Spain, were then considered a royal gift. Under the Habsburgs the Spanish school was started in Vienna, where the famous Lippizaner horses—originally a present to the Austrian emperor from a Turkish sultan—were shown to the Emperor and his Court. Vienna was then the home of *haute école,* and from Vienna it spread all over the Continent and was introduced into England by that great lover of horses and expert horseman, the Duke of Newcastle. Whilst training in dressage was continued and improved

(*a*) Rotary movements of first one arm, then the other, and finally both. To be executed in a walk, trot and canter with and without stirrups and finally bareback

(*b*) Both arms outstretched horizontally, turning as far as possible *without releasing the knee-grip*

(c) After lying on horse's back, return to normal position, then lean forward and down, touching first left foot and then right with *both* hands, *without* losing knee-grip. The object of these exercises is to gain freedom, and knee-grip must at no time be lost

(d) Same exercise as in (c) showing the forward incline position. To be executed in a walk, trot and canter

(e) Turning in the saddle.
To be executed in a walk, trot and canter on both leads.
First movement—throwing over right leg and sitting with both legs on the near side.

Second movement—Position facing the horse's tail. Both positions must be
maintained for a few strides

E. Wertheimer

(*a*) The rider is allowed for the first time to hold the reins when jumping. Reins must be very long and loose

E. Wertheimer

(*b*) Reins are already half-shortened

(*c*) Reins have been further shortened but the rider has still not gained contact with the horse's mouth

(*d*) The rider has now full contact with the horse's mouth but allows the horse perfect freedom of head. Neither horse's action nor rider's position has changed in the least during all these exercises

E. Wertheimer

A correct modern saddle should allow the rider to jump without stirrups or reins

TRAINING OF THE HORSE

Method of training young horses to jump *without* interfering with their mouth. The horse uses its neck for balance as an athlete uses his arms when jumping. By applying the 'placing jump' (cavalette) the horse is made to jump off at the correct distance from the obstacle

(*a*) Horse going over placing jump after having approached at a trot

(*b*) Horse, having landed and taken one stride, taking the second before jumping off

(c) Jumping off point for real obstacle after exactly two strides

(d) Well over the jump

upon in Continental cavalry schools, in England it soon fell into disuse and was only recently revived by such enthusiasts as Lieutenant-Colonel Hance, Mr. Wynmalen and the organisers of the Bishop's Stortford shows. A man who is capable of making a fine dressage horse out of a green horse is a very fine horseman indeed; anyone should be proud to learn from him, for his skill is the result of many years of hard, patient work.

I have said before that elementary dressage at least is essential to the training of the show jumper. This must not be confused with what is known in England as 'schooling', which is used for the training of hacks, for there is no similarity whatever between the two. No one who sits in the hack or hunter seat could ever teach a horse to do anything but walk, trot and canter, all of which the horse knew long before the rider did.

This book deals only with show jumping, but there are several excellent books on dressage for those who are interested. In fig. 3 the reader will find an elementary dressage test, which is quite adequate for a future show horse.

I mentioned earlier that the training of a show horse seems very similar to that of a show rider. I would, however, stress that a beginner should never try to train a green horse, nor should he try to learn on a green horse, for neither will learn anything from the other. There must be an experienced horseman standing by to point out the mistakes that the beginner is making.

(1) Take the horse into the closed manège and then walk it round several times to acquaint it with the dimensions of the manège.

(2) Place one brightly-painted heavy pole on the ground and start walking over it, always with loose reins. After a dozen such rounds, place another pole on the other side of the manège—then one more at each narrow end.

(3) Now start trotting on loose reins over these poles, a dozen times in each direction. The horse will think nothing of it.

(4) Now place a brick under each end of the poles, thereby

raising it four and a half inches from the ground. Walk and then trot over the poles a dozen times in each direction but never give your horse the slightest indication of what he should do; *let him find his own way.*

(5) Start in a slow canter for several rounds in each direction.

(6) The next day start off with one brick under the poles, but after ten rounds in each direction put another brick under the poles, thus raising the jump to 9 in.

(7) Trot over the poles for ten rounds on each side, and repeat this for several days before raising the poles again.

(8) Now raise the poles again by means of another brick. They should now be about one foot off the ground. Walk, trot and canter over them for an hour.

(9) The next day place another pole on the ground in front of the raised first pole. Walk, trot and canter over the double poles.

(10) Repeat this for several days and then separate the two poles by 6 in. Walk, trot and canter over them.

(11) Now raise the poles, which have hitherto been on the ground, 4½ in. by means of bricks. Walk, trot and canter over them for a few days.

(12) Now raise both poles by means of another brick and spread them apart by a foot. Walk, trot and canter over them for a few days.

(13) Raise them again and spread them apart again, always taking your horse over them on perfectly loose reins.

This procedure must be carried out slowly, without rushing the horse, and, above all, without giving it the feeling that is it doing anything unusual. This sort of jumping should be the same to the horse as hopping over a tree branch on the ground in the open. As this exercise is not, strictly speaking, jumping it can be kept up every day for at least three-quarters of an hour and doesn't harm the horse in the least. It merely teaches the horse to look more carefully at the ground and pick up its legs. Never punish it or call it to attention if it stumbles over the poles and knocks them down—this will only make it conscious that something unusual is being demanded of it. Let it carry on as before and you will see that the next jump it will hop over with a foot to spare. But always remember to REWARD your horse as soon as you have finished working in the manège, with a handful of sugar or carrots. This is of the utmost importance because the horse should get used to the idea that after every effort it makes, however small, it will be rewarded and never punished. Thus it will do its work willingly and NOT under duress.

When, after about a month, the jumps have reached a height of 2 ft. 6 in. with a spread of 3 ft., carry on at this height until the horse can trot over them half asleep, with its head stretched forward and thinking nothing of them at all. The tendency of modern training is to get the horse used to jumping without once calling it to attention and, needless to say, without punishing it. When the jumps have reached a height of 3 ft. with a depth of 3 ft., don't jump the horse over them for more than twenty minutes at a time. The higher the jumps, the less the horse must be jumped over them. The longer you keep it over low jumps the better, and the more time you give it for the development of those groups of muscles which it does not naturally possess, the stronger will it become. A horse which has been trained slowly and never jumped higher than 3 ft. 6 in. in a year will stand up easily to twelve years' good show jumping. I have seen several excellent show jumpers which were over twenty years of age.

Use only a soft, flexible rubber snaffle and a drop noseband for training your horse in the manège. It may happen that the horse will jump a little faster and the rider may be 'left behind' and jerk the horse's mouth. With a rubber snaffle the horse will not feel much, but with an ordinary snaffle you may hurt it and make it aware that it may get hurt in the mouth when jumping. Once a horse realises this it will instinctively throw up its head when jumping to prevent its mouth from being hurt. It may even develop into a 'stargazer' if the rider has bad hands.

When the jumps have reached a height of 2 ft. 6 in. stop cantering your horse over them and only trot from then on. This is very important, as the green horse cannot judge the depth of a jump.

(1) Start raising the height of the jumps very slowly again— 2 in. every third day until the jumps have reached a height which the horse can no longer clear from a slow trot. It will then quite instinctively put in one or two gallop strides, as in the training of the novice rider.

(2) From that day onwards your horse has learned to judge for itself the height and depth of a jump, and has, moreover, learned this without the help of the rider and without being aware that it was jumping.

I have already mentioned that a horse's eyes are focused differently to those of human beings. Jumping is unnatural to it and it has to learn gradually how to size up the height and depth of an obstacle in order to be able to clear it with comfort.

(3) Raise the jumps slowly as before and let your horse pick its own footing in the jumps. If it needs a gallop stride before jumping, let it have its own way; if it can still trot over the jumps so much the better.

Trotting jumps are hard on the rider as he has to sit correctly and at the same time give the horse all the freedom of mouth it requires. They are, however, all-important in muscling-up your horse. There cannot be a better training for developing the jumping muscles of a horse than this slow, gradual raising of the jumps.

Many experts believe in lunging a horse over jumps or chasing it round a circular jumping lane. Personally I don't approve of these methods because I consider that they tend to make the horse conscious of jumping and at the same time reluctant to jump. You must use a whip to make a horse jump on a lunge or over a lane, and the whip will create the impression in a young horse that jumping is a sort of punishment. Furthermore, why make your horse do something in the beginning that it will never have to do later on, for example, jumping without a rider? This will only teach it bad habits, such as jumping out of its paddock into the road or into your neighbour's field. Therefore train your horse from the very beginning in the way it should go —that is, with a rider on its back. In the first place, it muscles-up the horse far better to have to carry a good weight over the jumps and, secondly, the horse is still under the impression that it is doing nothing out of the ordinary. The horse should have been lunged when broken to the saddle and trained in elementary dressage, but this should be stopped once the horse has started jumping training.

I should like to mention here that I am giving only the training for jumping. It stands to reason that the horse must be rested at regular intervals and should be left out in the open for several days. Over-training is as bad as under-training.

When the horse can no longer clear the jumps in a trot and starts putting in gallop strides of its own accord the second phase of its training begins—that is, the gallop jump. Here, again, as in the training of the novice rider we use the cavalette, which I have called the placing jump because that is its actual function.

(1) Place a low cavalette 35 ft. in front of a 3 ft. 6 in. jump and trot into this placing jump, then give slight leg pressure to make the horse take two gallop strides and jump. This is the only correct way of teaching your horse when to take off automatically.

Expert trainers, such as Lieutenant-Colonel Chamberlin,[1] of Fort Riley, Kansas, have in earlier days advocated different ways of making the horse 'stand back in the jump', as it is technically called. Chamberlin advocated putting an iron bar one foot in front

[1] See *Training Hunters, Jumpers and Hacks*, by Lieutenant-Colonel H. D. Chamberlin (Hurst & Blackett).

of the jump (which might be a wall, for instance), and at the same height as the jump. I maintain, however, that the horse cannot possibly see this iron bar and will hurt its shin bones against it and immediately become aware of something unpleasant while jumping. This may have the effect of making it jump a little higher, but it will make it miscalculate the jump altogether.

I achieved the desired effect in South America by the simple method of placing the horse correctly into the jump—that is,

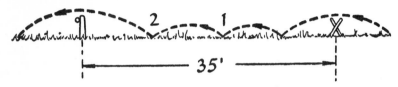

Fig. 2.—ERECTION OF THE PLACING JUMP:
(a) To give the horse *two* gallop strides: 35 ft. away.

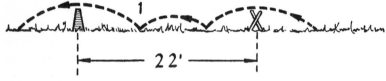

(b) To give the horse *one* gallop stride: 22 ft. away.

by putting a placing jump 35 ft. away from the real jump, which gave the horse exactly two strides and jump, neither more nor less. The horse was therefore able to clear the jump without being hurt as it hardly noticed that it was jumping. Horses trained in this manner never need rapping in the old-fashioned way, and the value of the training has been proved by the successes achieved in recent international events.

(2) Trot into the placing jump and let the horse gallop over the reduced and measured distance, and it will automatically describe the correct parabola over this jump with scarcely any effort at all.

(3) Repeat this for a dozen rounds or so and then place another jump on the other side of the manège (a vertical

one, as in the training of the rider) and place a cavalette 35 ft. in front of this second jump.

(4) From here on, take your horse into the paddock only twice a week and keep the jumps at a height of 3 ft.

(5) Now place another jump 35 ft. behind the first and make your horse jump two jumps in succession.

(6) Do the same thing on the other side of the manège.

(7) Vary the distance between the jumps—first 35 ft., then only 22 ft., and so on, to change the horse's strides continually.

After a couple of weeks of this take your horse only once a week into the manège and don't jump it more often. On the other days simply take it out for a ride and make it go over the trotting lane a couple of times every day.

This trotting lane is excellent exercise for the horse, as it will make it step higher and more carefully. In construction it resembles a long stepladder raised 8 in. off the ground and with a distance of 4 ft. between steps. It should be 8 ft. wide so that the horse does not try to leap out of it but trots through its whole length. There should be 10 to 15 poles in it, not more. Bring your horse into the lane in a trot, hold it slightly collected, and let it trot through. You will observe that it lifts its legs very high and carefully, and with the appearance of the dressage movement called 'passage' (see photo, *The Trotting Lane,* facing page 100). This must not be confused with what is usually called 'passage' in English-speaking countries, which is only a traverse, or work on two tracks.

(8) Vary the structure of the jumps—from vertical ones to spread jumps, and vary the spreads, too.

(9) When the height of the jumps has reached 3 ft. 6 in. the cavalette can be replaced by a low brush, low bar, or low wall. It must always be low and have no spread, and must not be higher than 2 ft. 6 in. to start.

After a few months of this training the horse must be taken into the jumping lane, the same as the novice rider. Keep the jumps in the lane low for as long as possible—you don't want your horse only for a couple of shows but for many years, and the longer it trains over low obstacles the stronger it will become. The exercises are exactly the same as in the training of the novice rider, except that the rider just sits normally and need not take his feet out of the stirrups, nor drop the reins as long as he leaves the horse's mouth free.

After a few months of this take the horse back into the manège, and start by giving it a few 4 ft. jumps with the placing jump. Then comes the next stage of its training—the gallop jump without the placing jump.

(1) Put up a single 2 ft. 6 in. jump on one side of the manège and start off in a slow, easy canter, allowing the horse to take this low jump in its stride.

(2) Place another jump on the other side of the manège and carry on with this exercise for a few weeks, slowly raising the jumps until after a month the horse can easily jump a height of 3 ft. 6 in. with a spread gradually increased to 4 ft. in depth. All these exercises must be executed on loose reins.

(3) From this stage onwards jump your horse only once a fortnight, and never forget to reward it generously.

(4) Increase the height and depth of these two single jumps up to 4 ft. by 5 ft., but not higher. A horse which can jump 4 ft. easily can, with equal ease, jump 4 ft. 6 in. and higher if necessary, as its muscles have already been developed, and it need make only a slight additional effort.

When the horse has reached this stage it has learned how to size up a jump by itself and has done so gradually, and without being aware that it has been doing something unpleasant.

After a couple of months of this, take your horse out into the open field; this is the last stage of the horse's training.

Put up the same course as that used for juveniles or pre-novices, and take your horse over it, controlling its speed and keeping constant though gentle contact with its mouth.

From now on jump your horse once every three weeks over such a course as this, but only once. If your horse jumps well and without making any faults, reward it with a handful of sugar, or carrots, but don't make it repeat a job it has already done well.

Vary this work by taking the horse every second time back into the manège and making it take ten to fifteen 3 ft. 6 in. jumps in a trot to keep its muscles in shape.

After a few months take it again into the jumping manège and raise the jumps to the height of an ordinary novice course, with the corresponding number of jumps. If the horse goes over smoothly, as it probably will, reward it but don't make it repeat the exercise. Do not on any account make it jump over a 4 ft. course when the highest jump in a novice course is 3 ft. 9 in. This is the only real difference in the training of horse and rider; it is of the utmost importance. A horse should never be forced to jump higher than it need; it is absolutely wrong to think that a horse which can jump over a 4 ft. course will take a 3 ft. 6 in. course at the same height and thus be certain of not knocking down a jump. A horse has far too much sense to make an exaggerated effort if there is no necessity for one. If it did, first category horses would have to jump more than 6 ft. to be sure of not making mistakes over a 5 ft. 3 in. course; high jumpers would have to clear 8 ft. to be sure of clearing a 7 ft. jump, and so on. A horse, like an athlete, is never the same from one day to the next—its physical condition varies exactly as ours does. It will have good and bad days, so don't try to force it to repeat an exceptional performance. Horses are flesh and blood, not machines.

Only now is your horse ready for its first show, and no sooner. From now on it does not need any more intensive training, but may be allowed to rest between shows. If the shows are very far apart, take it into the manège from time to time and give it a dozen 4 ft. trotting jumps and then a few jumps in the jumping paddock.

AN ALTERNATIVE METHOD OF TRAINING

Disconcerting results of a new method accidentally discovered lately.

I come now to a very important chapter, so important that it has practically warranted a new edition of this book—an alternative method of training the horse!

Just as I discovered many years ago by using a cine-camera in slow motion all the faults the rider commits in a show ring or in training, I have very recently discovered a new method of preparing a show jumper, which speeds up the training greatly.

After a bad fall I sustained a dangerous back injury, which altogether prevented me from jumping. I then decided to dedicate myself only to dressage, but lately even this strenuous exercise, although not as hard as jumping, would cause me great pain and I had to give it up also. All that was left to me then as far as riding was concerned, was simple work in the paddock or in the country in the easiest sort of seat I could accustom myself to. As I breed horses and never sell them, I have to ride several of them a day; all my horses are about fifty years younger than I am, well fed and therefore frisky as can be. Thoroughbreds are notoriously lazy when made to work in a closed-in ring, and thus give little work in comparison to other horses. So I have been doing nothing more than trotting and cantering slowly around the ring, avoiding all effort, so as to give me and the horses just enough exercise to keep fit.

Then I made a startling discovery—my Thoroughbred horses, instead of turning soft and lazy, became every day more powerful and developed exceptional muscles where they had none earlier! When, after working them in this manner (I cannot call it training), I had those horses go over a few jumps, I noticed to my surprise that they could jump very high after only a few months of this work!

I shall describe here this sort of training, for such I can call it now, but I would like to state that I still consider it somewhat unorthodox, although the results are amazing. By applying this new method I have obtained exactly the same results if not far better ones, in less than half the time of the conventional methods I have advocated earlier in this book. I shall analyse now the results obtained by this method:

(1) This method will give in a very short time to the raw horse, to the nervous Thoroughbred just off the race track, to the careless horse inclined to stumble often, to the horse with an iron mouth, to the horse with the wrong head carriage (star-gazer) what it needs indespensably for show jumping: a perfect natural balance, which a horse could earlier only gain by months and years often, of hard dressage work. Without having such a natural balance, no horse is really ready to partake in a show.

(2) Thoroughbreds, which I had taken out of races to use as hacks, who could do nothing else but gallop, and were quite naturally completely thrown off balance when carrying double the weight they were used to, very soon developed secure forelegs, tremendous muscles on chest, arms and hindquarters, and gained a perfect balance which only years of dressage work could have given them.

(3) Horses with the wrong head carriage, U-necks or a cast-iron mouth, very soon gained a perfectly normal head carriage, and a normally sensitive mouth.

(4) Finally careless horses who used to stumble at every pace and often crash to their knees, became as sure-footed as mules in an amazingly short time, and became elastic and springy where they had been sorrily sluggish in their movements earlier.

The only two conditions necessary for this sort of training are:

(1) A *small* paddock, well fenced in on all sides and about 50

× 75 ft. in dimensions (18–19 metres by about 23 metres long).

(2) A *heavy* rider, anything up to 225 lb. with saddle and all (100 kilos).

If the reader disposes only of a larger paddock, it would cost little to fence up these dimensions, even by a movable or temporary fence. If the reader weighs little, this is also easily overcome by using a racing namna, with lead weights added to make up the weight needed.

There are also two factors of the utmost importance that must always be remembered:

(1) *A soft rubber snaffle* only must be used, without any contact even with the horse's mouth.

(2) The training must be done at the slowest possible speed, so slow that the horse would be inclined to fall into a walk from the slow trot and into a trot from the too slow gallop. If these two cardinal points are not applied rigorously, the effect could be to the contrary! A good horse may be ruined and often even injured and thus useless for jumping! The rest is so simple and easy as to sound almost silly and impossible.

I shall now give the exercises to be applied in this new method: Take your horse into the sort of ring I have described and walk around it for several rounds on a completely loose rein. When the horse has made up its mind that it cannot break out and that there is therefore no use in rushing, start trotting *very slowly* around on *completely loose reins* for ten rounds. Then change direction and walk one round only. Then continue for another ten rounds with always one round walk in between, and thus up to eighty rounds altogether. Then walk several rounds only, to rest the horse and your legs, for it will take legs to keep your horse from not falling back into a walk all the time, so bored will it become with the monotonous work.

Then begin again all over and canter, but as before, without any contact whatsoever with the horse's mouth. Should your horse start off too fast, check it naturally until it will canter slowly on loose reins; but to achieve this you must use your legs, as otherwise it will fall back into a trot.

In this manner also do eighty rounds of the slowest possible canter, then take your horse out, the work for the day is done. That is all there is to it!

Should your horse be young or weak, begin with fewer rounds naturally. Then after a week or so you can do your hundred and sixty rounds between trot and canter. When cantering around the narrower end of your ring, you can even lean backwards! The very contrary to all that modern training methods advise. This will speed up the muscling of the hindquarters and make the horse put his hindlegs well *under the belly,* exactly what we earlier obtained by months of patient dressage work. These hundred and sixty rounds represent about one hour's easy and slow work, sufficient as a days' work for any horse. Very soon you will discover the following amazing changes in your horse's behaviour:

(1) The horse which used to be a star-gazer or even have a U-neck, will every day carry its head *lower and lower,* even lower than its withers! and thus gain the natural head carriage it had as a foal but lost through the bad hands of its earlier riders. You will notice soon packets of new muscles where the neck starts, which after several months of this training will be so developed as to even prevent the horse from raising its head too high, or at least KEEP it that way for more than a few seconds.

(2) The clumsy and careless horse which used to stumble will become sure-footed like an old mule. True, in the first days it will stumble even more. It probably will even fall several times on its knees, but it won't get hurt in the soft sand of the paddock, nor could the rider fall off at so slow a speed. Now if the horse does

fall, throw away the reins and never try pulling it up when it is falling; don't even give it the slightest aid to recover from falling. Let it struggle by itself to its legs and just continue as before; it will soon be sturdy on its legs.

(3) The horse that was unbalanced, as most horses usually are which have not been given lengthy dressage work will in no time gain a perfectly natural balance, and thus overcome the handicap of the rider's weight on its long back by developing a completely new set of muscles where it had none earlier. In short, the horse will gain the balance which until now was only obtained by months and even years of dressage work.

(4) Your horse will very soon develop also what is indispensible for jumping—powerful hindquarters, a powerful chest and tremendous muscles on fore- and hindlegs, sturdy pastern and hock tendons, and it will thus become springy and very elastic in its movements.

(5) The horse with the hard mouth will very soon regain a normal mouth, after having no contact whatsoever with the reins for several months, which allows it to play continuously with its tongue and thus never have a dry mouth.

After a week of this easy work, the rider should place one cavalette on each side of the ring and continue trotting and cantering over at the slowest possible speed. After another week add one more cavalette on each side, but only distanced by 9 ft. from the other one, which will oblige the horse to BOUNCE only, as there is not enough space for the horse to put in one stride between the two cavalettes. After another week they should be removed and replaced by four or five (if the ring allows it) cavalettes placed in a line in the centre of the ring. After each twenty rounds the horse should be taken over those cavalettes thus making it BOUNCE only over them by separating them by no more than 9 ft.

Should the reader have some sort of alley, he should then place more cavalettes in line, varying the distances between them and the height or even taking one out so as to allow the horse one stride, but then force it to only bounce again. This is NOT jumping training. This sort of work is only excellent to give the horse elasticity and to make it springy. The rider must be the judge and decide if the horse is now what it ought to be, but I always advocate patience and more patience. With this sort of training though, the time for preparing, or should I say of making a horse ready and fit for jumping, is cut by more than half compared with all previous methods. All the horse needs after this sort of training is a couple of weeks' dressage work so as to regain a mouth which, along with the leg work, will finally give your horse the all-important balance *in* the show ring *between* the jumps.

I should like to mention a case and experience of my own. I took one of my fillies out of races as she had a great handicap— she was born in May and was thus fully five months younger than all the other fillies racing in her age group. This is nothing at all in horses over five years of age, but all-important in fillies, as it makes the world of a difference if a filly is seventeen or twenty-four months old when racing. It is the same comparatively as matching a boy of, let us say, ten against a boy of fourteen years of age. The above-mentioned filly was weak and lanky, had a bad U-neck and was very unsteady on her forelegs. I got to work on her straight away. Today I weigh, with saddle and all, almost 220 lb., and that filly had never carried more than 110 lb. in races! So in the first rounds she stumbled and fell to her knees in a slow trot or walk, but after only four months of this work she developed tremendously powerful forelegs, broad hindquarters and never once again stumbled, despite my great weight! For the first three months I only trotted her, but after that I made her canter also, but very slowly, of course. I sent her back to the races as a four-year-old and out of eight races she won five firsts and one second prize!

I also obtained exactly the same result with older Thoroughbreds, which had anything but the conformation and the making of good jumpers. After three months of this training they had become so strong and muscled-up that they easily cleared anything up to 6 ft. (1.80 metres) and, I admit, much to my own annoyance, for this simply overthrows all my earlier methods and theories.

RAPPING

I have always maintained and proved that rapping is absolutely useless, and quite cruel at times, especially if nail-studded bars are used or nail-studded poles tied firmly to the posts of a jump.[1] The idea seemed to be to make the horse 'respect' the obstacle —that seemed to be the reason why some trainers and horsemen have for many years rapped their horses with gadgets that were cruel to a greater or lesser extent. When the horse knocked down the poles of an obstacle too frequently they figured the horse had no respect for the jump. This never made sense to me; still less did it make horse-sense. First of all, no animal will respect anything it has to do against its will—something even against its nature, imposed upon it by man in most cases by brutality. Brutality has never engendered respect, and certainly never affection, but only hatred and latent rebellion which will break out at the first opportunity, in this case by refusing to jump or running out. If a horse continually knocks down easy-looking jumps it is always the rider's fault, never the horse's. By easy-looking jumps I mean jumps normally supplied in shows, 3 ft. to 5 ft. high.

When I began to study the action of horses when jumping, the first thing I noted was one that had apparently escaped other horsemen, who did not like the idea of their horses being careless and rapped them accordingly; I noticed that the horse liked being careless even less, that knocking its legs against a pole caused it unpleasant pain. After that I watched hundreds of horses jumping and soon saw that a normal horse, weighing around 1,000 lb.,

---

[1] Rapping, one is glad to note, is prohibited by the British Show-jumping Association and competitors found indulging in this practice are subject to disciplinary action.

which knocks its legs against a pole when jumping at 500 yards per minute suffers a very strong shock and often sharp pain— far more pain than a man could inflict with a bamboo cane, provided that cane was not studded with sharp nails. In any case, a man can effectively rap the horse only when it has cleared the jump without knocking down the pole, in which case it is quite illogical to rap it.

I went further and tried to find out for myself just how much pain one feels when knocking one's shinbones against a heavy pole. I used an ordinary 4 in. pole 18 ft. long, and deliberately jumped low so that I hit my legs against it. Well, I almost broke my neck and was laid up for a week! When I could get up again I repeated the performance, asking one of my friends to 'rap' me as I went over the jump. True, it hurt a lot but far less than when I knocked my legs against the heavy pole!

Having proved this fact, I tried to find out what made the horse knock against the poles so frequently, and I found to my surprise that the horse simply could not help it. I took a riderless horse into a jumping lane and made it go over a jump, watching it very carefully. It jumped just high enough to clear the jump— perhaps two inches higher—but it did not knock it down. I put an average rider on the same horse and noticed that the horse then knocked down the poles several times. Other experienced horsemen watching my experiment immediately put that down to the sudden weight on the horse's back, but having a somewhat controversial mind I refused to accept this easy explanation and carried on with my experiment. I strapped 250 lb. of lead on the same horse and made it jump again several times—the horse cleared the jump perfectly, every time. I am sure the reader has understood what happened at the actual moment of the jump; it was not the weight of the rider (in that instance only 175 lb.), but the shifting of the rider's weight on the horse's back which made it commit faults. Having established this important fact, I went even further. I built a dummy rider of leather and wire and strapped it firmly to a horse and made the horse jump. I then made the third discovery: that it did not matter in the least how the dummy sat on the horse when jumping as long as its weight did not shift. I first made the dummy sit inclined well forward at an angle of 45 degrees in a modern jumping seat; then perfectly upright, then leaning backwards at the same angle of 45 degrees. The horse jumped every time with equal ease. I repeated this experiment with several other horses, but the result was always the same. After that I knew for certain that it was the rider's fault if the horse knocked down a pole—never the horse's.

The next thing I tried to find out was why the rider shifted his weight at the moment of jumping. I asked hundreds of riders —novices and experienced ones—and every time got the same surprising answer—'To make it easier for the horse'.

One day I gathered together all the members of my riding club and repeated my experiment with the dummy rider for their benefit. They watched in silence and were absolutely amazed. The simple truth had apparently escaped everyone for as long as there had been show jumping. We then sat down and discussed this discovery and every rider finally admitted that he really rose in the stirrups and leaned forward over the horse's neck simply to make it possible for *him* to jump and remain on his horse—not, as he had believed, to make it easier for the horse. The riders tried over and over again and had to admit finally that they simply had to lean forward and rise out of the saddle at the moment of jumping, otherwise they were left badly 'behind' and almost toppled over their horse's back.

I left it at that for the moment, and continued to observe carefully the exact movements of the rider in the jump and realised that the human eye was not fast enough to ascertain accurately what the rider actually did, or how the horse reacted. I therefore got a cine-camera and filmed hundreds of riders when jumping, always employing the slow-motion speed, and then made my last and most surprising discovery: that every time the rider leaned forward and supported his upper body on the horse's neck—usually by simply bridging the reins—the horse's forehand automatically dropped by anything from 4 in. to 9 in. and thus frequently knocked down the pole! The contrary happened when the rider was 'left behind' and thus put too much weight on the horse's hindquarters; the hindlegs then dropped visibly by 4 in. to 9 in. and the horse again knocked down the pole. Then I filmed the dummy again over the same jumps and the horse cleared the obstacles with ease, no matter whether the dummy was inclined forward, placed upright or inclined backwards. What the rider apparently did was to shift his weight, suddenly placing anything from 20 lb. to 50 lb. extra weight on the horse's forehand—and this just at the crucial moment of the jump—the take-off. Again I called all the members of my riding club together and showed them the film. Everyone agreed then that it was the fault of the rider and never the horse if it failed to clear jumps. But they insisted that they simply could not sit like dummies without moving—and it was easy enough to discover why. The stomach muscles of a man are never strong enough to maintain the body in exactly the same position it was in when approaching the jump—that is, upright. Therefore, when the horse suddenly leapt away under the rider the rider had to fall backwards. To avoid this happening the rider instinctively leaned forward, anticipating and endeavouring to counteract the jerk. This made him attempt to 'place' the horse so that he would know when it was going to jump, so avoiding the jerk and being 'left behind'.

The first thing I condemned, therefore, was the 'placing' of the horse into the obstacle. But that alone did not eliminate the rider's difficulty, so I began to study how that difficulty could be overcome, how the rider could be made to sit quietly at the moment of jumping so as not to interfere with his horse's freedom of action. I very soon found the solution—a correctly built jumping saddle. Having solved that problem, I started to train riders in such a way that they remained in a position which combined the rider's comfortable and firm seat with the horse's freedom of action, so developing what I call the Modern Jumping Seat in the chapter entitled 'The Modern Seat for Show Jumping'.

When making further slow-motion films of horses in the act of jumping I noticed that they never cleared the jump by a wide margin but only by a few inches. This was a revelation to me and confirmed my strong belief in 'horse-sense'. It proved that the horse instinctively sized up the height of the jump correctly and consequently made the necessary muscular effort it needed to get over. When projecting the films I could see another very interesting point: every time the horse jumped it raised its fore-legs so much that its knees were higher than its elbows and in many cases when the jump was higher it even raised its hooves higher than its belly. Another and better proof of horse-sense.

The horse rose only high enough from the ground to clear the obstacle with its heaviest part—its body—by a couple of inches! It achieved this apparently by raising its forelegs as high as possible and tucking in its hindlegs.

Does it not stand to reason that if this is the easiest way for the horse to jump without a rider it should logically also be the best way with one? After all, if we want maximum effort from a horse we must also give it maximum freedom of movement and let it find the easiest way of getting its heavy body over an obstacle.

This discovery reminded me of an experience in my youth, when I used to indulge in all sorts of hard, physical exercises such as athletics. I used to be quite a good high-jumper then, and even established a record of some sort with 5 ft. 5 in. Being young, I was naturally mighty proud of my achievement and boasted no little about it until one day an English athlete came to our Academy to give us a demonstration of the modern technique in jumping. That day was certainly the darkest in my youth. My manly pride was shattered and with it all my little self-respect gone! That English chap, a weak and skinny-looking fellow, easily cleared 6 ft. 6 in.! After the first shock I was convinced that the fellow was somehow cheating, if only to excuse my own inadequacy, but to my sorrow I could find out only one thing: that he had applied a new and more efficient method. Instead of raising his whole body upright over the pole, and throwing first one leg and then the other over it, as we were taught to do, he 'rolled' over the pole. While I had to make a great effort and raise my whole upper body over 5 ft. 5 in., the lowest point being my buttocks, he made only a comparatively little effort to achieve the same result. When going over the pole his whole body was perfectly horizontal from toes to head. After I found that out I decided that what that skinny chap could do I could do far better, and I tried hard to imitate his style but never got much beyond badly twisting my wrist several times and once almost breaking my neck before I had to admit myself defeated and give up any further attempts to establish high-jump records.

Many years later, when observing horses jump, and when filming their movements, I remembered my high-jumping endeavours and once more realized that horses have quite a lot of 'horse-sense', apparently far more than the average youth. They instinctively did the right thing, just as the English athlete, and thus spared themselves unnecessary effort. Instead of raising the whole body they merely lifted their legs higher and thus did not waste energy. I immediately got busy on this discovery and tried to train my horses accordingly. As I had already eliminated the handicap of the rider's shifting weight by modern training, and by a correctly-built jumping saddle, I found out that all the horse needed from then on was absolute freedom of movement and vision. We all know that horses are long-sighted. Horses can see clearly several miles ahead but are practically blind at very short distances. The reader may try the following experiment to convince himself: hold a fresh carrot about eight inches away from the horse's eye and he will discover that the horse can smell it but cannot see it—and a horse cares far more for a carrot than for the prettiest jump! I deduced, therefore, that there was no sense in punishing a horse for presumed negligence when jumping when it simply could not see the obstacle clearly. This usually happened when the rider had slowed down his horse to a mere prancing pace and brought it too close under the jump, thus practically blindfolding it.

When we drive a car at thirty miles an hour we do not look right in front of the wheels but survey the road at least a hundred yards ahead. When we see an obstacle we detect it from a distance of a hundred yards and know exactly how to avoid it when reaching it, and do not need to slow down the car to a practical standstill to by-pass it. Exactly the same thing applies to the horse. When a horse approaches an obstacle at a certain speed it has already sized up the height and depth from a certain distance away, according to its speed, and it knows exactly what to do with its four legs, where to take off and what muscular effort to produce to get itself over the obstacle in the easiest possible way. Anything else the rider may do, apart from sitting correctly and encouraging the horse with leg pressure, would only handicap the horse's freedom of movement and vision. The only reason for which a rider slowed down his horse in front of an obstacle— supposedly to 'place' it and make it easier for the horse to jump —was actually to make it easier for himself. All he achieved by doing this was to confuse the horse, throw it off balance and commit faults. I changed all my training methods and from then on based them on making the horse *lift* its legs as high as possible and thus clear the jump with its belly with only a few inches to spare, instead of forcing a horse to overjump by several feet while allowing its legs to dangle. The heavier the horse, the more speed it naturally needs to get over a high and deep obstacle. If it is slowed down too much it cannot use its four sound legs any longer, but only two, its hindlegs. Nature provided a horse with four legs and not with two like the kangaroo. There is no sense, there-fore, in making a horse use only its hindlegs, jump off the hocks when it can achieve the same result with far less effort through more speed.

It is quite easy to train a green horse to jump correctly. It will do it instinctively if allowed, but to get a horse out of bad habits is almost as difficult as to re-train a rider who has jumped a great deal already and got into the bad habit of 'placing' his horse. I will give here the method of making a horse jump correctly again after having previously been ruined—made to jump always 'off its hocks' in a 'cat jump', and thus handicapped in getting over deep oxers and triple bars or combined jumps.

As in the ordinary training, the horse must be trained with the placing jump. Erect a 4 ft. gate and then put a low placing jump 30 ft. away from it. Then trot slowly to the placing jump and once over, giving leg-pressure to get from a trot into a canter. The horse will make two strides and jump. Gradually increase the distance from 30 ft. to 45 ft. (Note that this is longer by 5 ft. than any distance applied in show courses.) The horse will then gradually stand back more and more as the speed of approach remains the same, but the distance is gradually increased from 30 ft. to 45 ft. In the opposite case, when a horse is inclined to 'stand back' too much into the jumps and thus 'jumps wildly', the procedure should be reversed. The maximum distance of 45 ft. must be applied to begin with and then gradually reduced to 30 ft.

I have trained hundreds of horses in this manner and have never failed to achieve the desired result. But there is an all-important factor necessary for this sort of training; patience and more patience. There is no sense whatever in rapping the horse to make it jump better and higher. All the horse needs to jump is:

(1) Speed.
(2) A free neck so that it can see the obstacle correctly.
(3) A certain amount of encouragement from the rider. (Nervous riders make nervous horses.)
(4) Encouragement but NOT punishment. There is no sense in punishing a horse for the rider's mistakes.

The worst thing a rider can possibly do is to slow down his horse. This he can do only by pulling on the reins and the horse's mouth, thus shortening the horse's neck and depriving it of its only means of balance. It is exactly the same as strapping an athlete's arms behind his back and asking him to establish a record high jump! Just as the athlete needs his arms to balance himself, so does the horse need absolute freedom of its neck to balance and jump correctly and 'bascule' (arch) itself freely over the jump.

I want to mention here another experiment I made with a young horse, first handled and ridden by me and trained by me. I wanted to prove that jumping is an unnatural movement to the horse, but that any horse could become a good jumper if it were trained in such a manner that it did not realise that it was doing anything unnatural. I trained it in the manner explained in the chapter on training the young horse, but every time it jumped I rewarded it generously with a good double handful of sugar, whether it did well or not. I never once used a whip on the training, maintaining that the moment the horse was punished it would associate jumping with pain. The result was amazing. After some months of this training the horse would think of only one thing: to get as fast as possible into the jumping paddock and look round for a jump to leap over! Jumps became its obsession. When I took that horse out into the open it would still be looking for something to jump over, and when it encountered a hunt jump, wall or garden fence it would make off at a gallop and jump happily over it, then stop, look back and ask me for the sugar! I could go with that horse into a huge open field with one solitary jump erected in the centre and it would immediately make a bee-line for the obstacle and jump it. But that same horse which passed its time looking for obstacles to jump never once jumped over the low, 3-ft. rails of the grazing paddock simply because I never once made it jump without a rider on its back. This is the reason why I strongly advocate NOT making horses jump without a rider; it teaches them bad habits and serves no real purpose at all.

Chapter Three

Shows and Courses

The classification of show riders and show horses is derived from the old and intelligent way of handicapping Thoroughbreds in races. In the same way as our sport this way of classification has come from England with its traditional 'fair-play' in all sports. Just as racehorses can race in four different handicaps according to the prizes they have won, show horses were supposed to be similarly protected.

Thus a horse which is too young, or has not won any races, can be entered in the fourth category of a given handicap, so as to have a fair chance to win, running only against horses of a similar category. So far so good; now this simple and most efficient way of classification is being adopted in every country in a different manner, surprising though this may sound, and all under the auspices of the International Federation! In fact the result is sheer chaos, with a few practical exceptions. The International Federation seems, in my opinion, to wash its hands of the whole business and leave the classification entirely to the criterion of the National Federations.

In Spain, for instance, I found out that there are NO classifications whatsoever as far as novices or open riders are concerned. The difference seems to be based on the winnings! Any horse which has won over a thousand pesetas (£6 or 75 SM) gets a handicap, which is applied by simply making that horse jump a few jumps higher, usually raised by 4 in. (10 centimetres) but over the same course. On the other hand any horse or rider could enter for the usual two events in a Spanish show: a lower category with perhaps only two double obstacles and a higher one with a few jumps raised by 4 to 6 in. (10 to 15 centimetres). This does not make sense at all to me. Why the two different events if anyone can enter for both? In Spain I also found another great paradox. Whereas the United States decided horses were not necessary for the officers being trained in their Army Colleges and were too expensive to be kept, some Continental countries seem to buy every year lots of horses from Ireland and France for just one purpose—show jumping. I have seen even lieutenants and captains anything but outstanding in their performance, being issued with even TWO such very expensive horses so as to partake in the frolics of show jumping! I know personally such officers who rode very poorly in my opinion, but were using horses which had cost the country over £1,500 each! I have also known officers who had won in shows anything up to £2,000 in one year! And that on free horses for which they don't even pay one penny for upkeep. I don't know if I am mistaken but I was under the impression that winning a lot of money in a sport made a professional out of a so-called amateur. A real amateur, as keen as he may be for jumping, has in my humble opinion a very poor chance against these gentlemen, as praiseworthy as their Government's effort towards equestrian sports may be.

In France I found another sort of classification, far more logical and certainly very practical.

The clever French make no pretence whatsoever about their intentions and clearly are out for business—horse breeding. They classify all their horses by their age-group. Their classification is the following:

(1) Jumping events for 4-year-old horses BORN and raised in France.

(2) Jumping events for 5-year-old horses BORN and raised in France.

(3) Jumping events for 6-year-old horses BORN and raised in France.

All those events are judged WITHOUT THE CHRONOMETER, that is speed does NOT COUNT (a very sensible rule in my humble opinion). If there happen to be three or even seven competitors with an equal number of faults, they are automatically all winners Ex-Equo.

(4) Events for horses in the age group 7–12 also for French bred and raised horses. All horses which have passed twelve years of age cannot jump any longer in any shows in France with the sole exception of International Shows! The same goes also for foreign horses wanting to jump in France, they can ONLY take part in the International events.

We all know that horse breeding is a very expensive business or hobby, and the logical French seem to have understood this well, hence their clever classifications which for all purposes eliminates foreign horses and helps enormously the hard-pressed breeders.

In some English-speaking countries I have discovered even greater paradoxes. I helped organise horse shows in a British dominion and was immediately confronted with the wellnigh impossible task of classifying the riders or their horses. I was shown for instance, for my guidance, the regulations ruling such shows and cite here a couple for the reader to figure out.

1. *The definition of a Novice rider* [*sic*]

'. . . a novice rider will be taken to mean a person who, at the time of entering the ring, has never won a First,

Second or Third prize in a Novice or OPEN [*sic*] jumping
event, at any of this Society's Shows'.

First of all they mentioned 'OPEN EVENTS' in which, in my
opinion a novice has no business to be in. Otherwise there is no
sense in having novice events at all if that same novice deems
himself capable of also jumping in open events, which I take are
far more difficult.

Secondly, they emphasised 'of THIS Society's Shows'! Now I
discovered *three more* such societies in that same country! All of
them must have had apparently similar or different rules.

When I threw up my hands and insisted I could never reach
a sensible classification under such conditions, they suggested a
truly Solomonic decision—'*Restricted Events*'.

They suggested that the courses I put up should be called
thus, and went on to define the meaning of this ominous Restricted;
it turned out to be another puzzle, and not as I had feared at
first restricted as far as the pigmentation of the skin of the riders
or their religious aberrations were concerned. The cryptical
definition of that event was thus expounded:

2. *Restricted Events*

'. . . with the Exception of the Grand Prix (apparently
open to novice riders) [*sic*] are open only to riders who
have won a First, Second or Third Prize in an individual
adult Jumping event at a Central Show or a First Prize,
at any show held under auspices of —— Horse Showing
Association'.

A Central Show was explained as follows:

'Central Shows shall be deemed to be those held annually
in —— [the towns of the aforementioned three Societies]
where Annual Agricultural Shows are held'.

This conveyed to me the impression that there were still
OTHER similar bodies, whose shows were considered somewhat

E. Wertheimer

Always jump young horses on loose reins to allow maximum freedom. Use only a soft rubber snaffle or the horse may get into the bad habit of throwing up its head at the moment of jumping

E. Wertheimer

THE TROTTING LANE. An excellent training for young horses, often careless with their forelegs. It will make them very attentive and cause them to raise the forelegs

E. Wertheimer

(*a*) Comfortable and very firm seat on correctly built modern saddle. Horse has perfect freedom of movement, particularly with forelegs—knees higher than elbows

(*b*) Compelled to seek extra support by bridging reins, as saddle does not give sufficient for a comfortable seat. The extra weight on the horse's neck forces its forelegs back under its belly

inferior to the first three, as only first-prize winners of those shows were deemed eligible for the restricted events.

(1) Combined Caprili or Three-Day Event.
(2) Novice Rider Event.
(3) Third Category Event.
(4) Second Category Event.
(5) First Category Event.
(6) Special Event for Third Category horses with riders of the First, Second and Third Categories.
(7) High Jump Event.
(8) Six-Bar Event.
(9) Broad Jump Event.
(10) Dressage Events—sub-divided into three categories (Elementary, Medium and First Category dressage tests).

(1) *The Combined Caprili or Three-Day Event*

This originated in Italy and has since been adopted by all countries as being the best test of horse and rider. It was elaborated by Frederico Caprili, as the name indicates, who was the father of modern equitation and cavalry training, and it is today the main event in all Olympic Games.

It consists of three different events:

(*a*) First Day—a cross-country of anything up to 22 miles.
(*b*) Second Day—a light dressage test.
(*c*) Third Day—a jumping event.

The cross-country race can be condensed into a point-to-point of 2 to 4 miles with an increased number of obstacles, but all of them of moderate height. The dressage test is easy—almost elementary—and is usually composed of 20 to 30 different movements. The jumping event corresponds to a modern Third

Category event, except that the speed is a little faster. The jumps, however, should be limited to 3 ft. 11 in.

Each event is judged separately, the total points being added to decide the winner. Although this event is supposed to be held on three consecutive days it can easily be fitted into one day. The point-to-point race should then be reduced to a race of 2 miles, held early in the morning; the dressage test can follow before lunch and the jumping in the afternoon.

(2) *Novice Rider Event*

Maximum Height, 4 ft. Speed Limit, 330 yards per minute.

Novice courses should have a maximum of eighteen jumps and a minimum of fourteen jumps. Of these only two jumps should be 4 ft. high and they should not be single jumps but the last of a group of three, preferably triple bars and hogs' backs.

A Novice course should consist of three obstacles of three jumps each, three obstacles of two jumps each and a few single jumps. The first, or entering, jump of a combined obstacle should always be easy and low, the other two each a little higher. Although it may seem to the reader difficult to jump a 4 ft. jump with only two strides' run it is actually far easier, since the horse is already correctly placed. The single jumps should be hog's backs, post and rails, and brushes, all of only moderate height. No water jump should be used.

(3) *Third Category Event*

Maximum Height, 4 ft. 4 in. Speed Limit, 400 yards per minute. Maximum Number of Jumps, 22. Minimum 17.

A Third Category course, being the next step from the Novice course, should quite naturally be an easy step and not much higher than a Novice course.

Three jumps only should be 4 ft. 4 in. high. One-third of the jumps should be 4 ft. high, and one-third should be spread jumps, with a maximum spread of 5 ft. for triple bars and 4 ft. 6 in. for oxers, parallel bars and hogs' backs. As in the Novice course, the highest jumps should always be the last in a combined obstacle of three jumps. For example:

Jump No. 13   Brush and rail   3 ft. 6 in. high
Jump No. 14   Wall   4 ft. high
Jump No. 15   Triple Bar   4 ft. 4 in. high

This way of building jumps should always be borne in mind by those erecting a modern course. A ten-foot water jump may be used in these events.

(4) *Second Category Events*

Maximum Height, 4 ft. 8 in. Speed Limit, 450 yards per minute. Maximum Number of Jumps 25. Minimum 18.

Second Category events are in modern show jumping what open events were in old-fashioned shows. The Third Category serves only as a means of letting the novice rider gain experience before being faced by higher courses. It also serves as a means of restraining over-enthusiastic riders from trying to fly before they can walk.

In these courses there should be a maximum of four 4 ft. 8 in. jumps which, as before, should always be placed last in an obstacle of three jumps. There should be about five 4 ft. 4 in. jumps, six 4 ft. jumps, and the rest under 4 ft.

(5) *First Category Events*

Maximum Height, 5 ft. 2 in. Speed Limit, 550 yards per minute. Maximum Number of Jumps, 30. Minimum, 22.

First Category events are exactly the same standard as the most difficult international events and the top events in the Olympic Games, the only difference being that in South America six to eight more obstacles are used, though the maximum height of these jumps is kept to 5 ft. 2 in.

One-third of the jumps must be spread jumps, with a maximum spread of 7 ft. In a course of twenty-three to twenty-eight jumps, five should be 5 ft. 2 in., another six 5 ft., about eight 4 ft. 8 in., another eight 4 ft. 4 in., and the rest 4 ft.

Obstacles should be constructed so as to rise gradually in height, as in previous courses. In Appendix Course F, Jumps No. 19, 20 and 21.

> Jump No. 19   Picket fence   4 ft. 4 in.
> Jump No. 20   Post and rails   4 ft. 6 in.
> Jump No. 21   Triple Bar (6 ft. deep) 4 ft. 8 in.

A rider who can negotiate such courses with only a few faults is ready for any international event or the *Prix des Nations* of the Olympic Games.

The reader will now easily understand why I have emphasised that only competent and expert men should be allowed to lay out a modern jumping course, as the slightest mistake in calculating the distances will make it practically impossible for the horse to get over the course, and may also cause grave accidents. Obviously the only really competent men for this task are top-category riders who have had to jump over such courses and know what is possible and what is recklessly dangerous.

The rider must always bear in mind the fact that his horse is already accurately placed and must think only of sitting correctly, giving his horse maximum freedom of mouth and loins and maximum pressure of legs when jumping. He must also remember never to look at the first jump in a number of jumps, but always at the last one so as not to be out of line in the middle or end.

(6) *Special Event for Third Category horses with rider of the First, Second and Third Categories*

This event is the modern version of the old-fashioned Novice Horse Class. Novice horses are not admitted into modern horse shows; they belong to a training manège until they are capable of smoothly negotiating the course of a Third Category Event. This special event is therefore intended to allow riders of the higher categories to bring up their new horses gradually. Usually the Third Category riders come first, then the jumps are slightly raised—though never more than three—and the Second Category riders follow. After another two or three jumps have been raised —though never higher than the maximum height of a Third Category Event—the First Category riders follow. The scoring is exactly the same as in other events, the better riders having been handicapped in advance.

(7) *The Six-Bar Event*

This event is one of the most popular ones in South America and has since spread all over the world. I have introduced it into many countries where it has now become a standing event in all horse shows.

As in a combined obstacle of two or three jumps, the six-bar event is considered as one single obstacle, which means that in the event of a refusal in the centre, or at the last jump, the whole six jumps must be taken again.

The six-bar event is composed of six post and rail jumps placed in a straight line, with the same distance between each jump. The horse is allowed only two strides and jump between jumps. I have already mentioned that the distance for two strides and jump varies from 35 ft. to 40 ft. (10.5 metres to 12 metres). It has proved very difficult to determine a correct speed limit for this event, as it is over practically as soon as it has started, and it has been found difficult to establish the corresponding distance between the jumps for each speed. In South America, where the average show jumper is not bigger than 15 hands, the difficulty has been overcome by imposing a fixed distance of 35 ft. (the minimum distance for two strides and jump) for this event, no time limit being applied. In countries like England, Ireland, the United States and Australia, where horses are usually over 16 hands, I would suggest using the maximum distance of 40 ft. between jumps.

This event should be restricted to Third, Second and First Category riders, as the jumps are rather high. Each jump is 4 in.

higher than the previous one, and each post and rails should have as many poles closely set together as possible, exactly like a high jump. They are disposed thus:

Jump No. 1	3 ft.
Jump No. 2	3 ft. 4 in.
Jump No. 3	3 ft. 8 in.
Jump No. 4	4 ft.
Jump No. 5	4 ft. 4 in.
Jump No. 6	4 ft. 8 in.

This is the first height, which all competitors have to negotiate. Those who get over without knocking down a jump can dismount, as in a high jump event, and wait until all competitors have negotiated the course.

Those riders who do not clear the course in the first trial have two more trials. If after the third trial they still fail to make a clear round they are eliminated, as in the high jump event.

The jumps are then all raised 4 in., being now the following heights:

Jump No. 1	3 ft. 4 in.
Jump No. 2	3 ft. 8 in.
Jump No. 3	4 ft.
Jump No. 4	4 ft. 4 in.
Jump No. 5	4 ft. 8 in.
Jump No. 6	5 ft.

Those riders who are still in the running go over again and, as before, have three trials. The jumps are then raised again, until all but a few riders have been eliminated. The scoring is as follows:

Knocking down Jump No. 1	6 faults
Knocking down Jump No. 2	5 faults
Knocking down Jump No. 3	4 faults
Knocking down Jump No. 4	3 faults
Knocking down Jump No. 5	2 faults
Knocking down Jump No. 6	1 fault

As in high jumping, the previous score is automatically annulled once the competitor has cleared a height. Only in the end, when none of the competitors succeeds in clearing the last height, is the previous score taken into consideration, and the one with the least number of faults is automatically the winner. This event is very spectacular and is an excellent test for horse and rider. It is almost precision jumping, as one second of slackening between two jumps may result in the rider losing the competition. It needs maximum concentration and split-second reflexes.

The rider must always remember the following important fact: the higher the jumps become, the shorter must be the horse's parabola over the jump. This means that each successive height the rider must keep his horse more and more in hand and collected, and must use his legs more every time and give the horse a check between each jump. Almost every time the horses are forced to jump off their hocks, and they develop great elasticity if the jumps are kept low for training, but as the jumps get higher the horse's effort must become more and more concentrated.

I am strongly against using a good show jumper for this event as it would ruin it. The reason is that in modern training we advocate longer and smoother parabolas in the jump, whereas the six-bar event tends to shorten the parabola and makes the horse jump off his hocks all the time. Special horses are used for the six-bar event in the Argentine, as it is constructed for horses who are not good over spread jumps. Similarly a horse which is good for the six-bar event is automatically an excellent horse for high jumping, and the best training for a higher jumper is over the six bars as it makes the horse very elastic and springy.

I had such a horse in the Argentine; it was unable to get over a Second Category course but won for me the six-bar event dozens of times. In fact, I think I still hold the world's record for that event, with 6 ft. 4 in. for the last jump.

A horseman, therefore, should never try to use the same

horse for six-bar events and high jump events, as well as broad jumps and ordinary courses. The champion high jumper in the Argentine, which held the record for many years with a jump of 7 ft. 11 in., could never get over a First Category course and only once won a Second Category event.

(8) *High Jump Event*[1]

The rules for this event have not been changed as the jump itself has remained unaltered; therefore I shall not enlarge upon it. I would mention only that the record was held for over twelve years by an Italian officer, Captain Gutiérrez, on Osopo, with a height of 2 metres, 44 centimetres—approximately 8 ft. 2½ in. Only recently this amazing record was broken by another 2 inches by a Chilean officer, the record jump being today 8 ft. 4½ in.

(9) *Broad Jump Event*

This is not as popular as the high jumping contest and in 1951 this record was broken by a Spanish officer, Lieutenant-Colonel Lopez de Hierro on Amado Mio—8.30 metres.

(10) *Dressage Classes*

Dressage classes are held regularly every week-end in all South American countries, as on the Continent. I need not emphasise again the great importance of such events, having already explained that they are absolutely essential training for any horseman who hopes to reach a high category in show jumping.

Dressage classes are divided into three:

(1) Light Dressage Test.
(2) Medium Dressage Test.
(3) Advanced Dressage Test.

As I mentioned earlier, the French being practically the first to begin again with horse shows, having by Colonel Cavaillé's

---

[1] The record for the High Jump in Great Britain was created by Swank at the International Horse Show, Olympia, in 1937. Ridden by Donald Beard, Swank cleared 7 ft. 6¼ in.

DIFFERENCE IN TRAINING METHODS
DICTATED BY QUALITY OF MOUNT

L'année hippique suisse, Lausanne, From the "Horseman's Year"

The rider is forced to gain extra support on his horse's neck for lack of a correctly built saddle. The result is his horse practically has to do a high jump to clear a five foot jump

Photo Rotondo, Buenos Aires

This rider sitting on a correct saddle has a firm seat and does not need to lean on his horse's neck for support and thus allows his horse the fullest freedom of movement. As a result this horse is making far less effort to clear the same height, the lowest part of his body being his belly.

Photo Rotondo, Buenos Aires

Captain Pistarini, Argentine Cavalry, on twenty-year-old *Brujo*, clearing 7 ft. 10 in.
Rider's position and horse's movements are almost identical with those in the last
photograph. This horse held the South American high jump record (then 7 ft. 11 in.)
for no fewer than 15 years

E. Wertheimer

Miss Heather Carruthers on *Westwood* demonstrates how high a horse can be made to
raise its forelegs if trained correctly and allowed absolute freedom of
shoulders and mouth

efforts saved a considerable number of excellent horses from the butcher's knife, were also quite naturally those who exercised the most influence on the International Equestrian Federation as far as officially recognised events were concerned.

Very soon their organisation of events imposed itself on most Continental countries where jumping events were held. Those typical French events have now been officially adopted by the F.E.I. as standards for all jumping events. They are:

(1) *Normal Jumping Events* (Epreuves normales)

Under this category fall events usually used in shows and are judged under *Bareme A*. (The definition of the various Baremes follows on page 126.)

(2) *Puissance*

This event consists of only six to eight obstacles, all VERTICALS with the exception of No. 1 jump, and all of a minimum height of 4 ft. 8 in. (1.40 metres). With each elimination a couple of jumps must be taken out and the remainder raised. For the last elimination there must be at least TWO jumps left, one a vertical and the other one a jump with depth, usually an Oxer. This event is also judged under *Bareme A*. But time is never taken into consideration.

(3) *Parcours de Chasse* (Hunting course)

This event consists of a makeshift hunting field. The obstacles are many and disposed in a complicated manner so as to gain maximum flexibility and agility from the horse. These events are judged under *Bareme B and C*. Time is considered.

(4) *Parcours Americain* (American event)

This event consists of only single NOT combined obstacles and is judged by the chronometer speed. The winner in such events can be decided in two ways: (a) With the number of maximum jumps stipulated in advance; (b) The riders must try to negotiate without faults a maximum number of obstacles in a specified fixed time.

Several relay events are also included, which are judged under a variety of rules left usually to the criteria of the organisers.

(5) *Prix des Nations*

This is an event only for teams of various nations and can only be called such if there are at least THREE international teams participating. Each team must be composed of FOUR riders and horses. Only in case of proven incapacitation of one of the participants can another one be allowed to jump TWO horses of that team. Only thirteen to fourteen obstacles are used in these events of no more than sixteen to twenty jumps. Height must be between 4 ft. 4 in. (1.30 metres) and 5 ft. 4 in. (1.60 metres) and the water jump must be at least 13 ft. wide (4 metres).

Only recently, in 1953, three new events have been accepted by the F.E.I. and are disputed every year:

(1) *World Champion for Show Jumping*
(2) *Continental Championship for Show Jumping*
(3) *Continental Championship for Junior Riders*

The F.E.I. organises every four years a World Championship in show jumping which must be held on the Continent in which Olympic games are being staged that year, but not in the same town or country.

The F.E.I. also permits national federations to stage every other TWO years world championship shows, the conditions for both events being that at least FIVE nations are participating in them. Another condition for the second event is that the organising country must invite the former world champion and the second of that event to participate. The National Federation have also the privilege of staging those championships in the country that holds at that time the World Champion, the next choice goes to the second man of any other nation.

These events are composed as follows:

1. Course designed for speed and manœuvrability.
2. A Course for Puissance.
3. Course as used in the *Prix des Nations*.
4. Final decided between the individual winners of each of the previous events. The height for the first event is between 4 ft. 4 in. (1.30 metres) and 5 ft. (1.50 metres). In the second event from 4 ft. 4 in. to 5 ft. 8 in. (1.30 to 1.70 metres).

This World Championship event was held for the first time in 1953 in Paris when the Spaniard Francisco Goyoaga won it on Quorum. The last world championship was won by David Broome on Mister Softee.

(2) *Continental or European Championship Event*
This event is staged every year except the years of the Olympic games. It is held under the same conditions as the World Championship, over similar courses with similar heights.

(3) *Junior Continental or European Championship Event*
These events are also held every year during the summer vacations and are restricted to junior horsemen up to seventeen years of age. It is composed, as in the other championships, of several events, but the height of the obstacles must be held at 4 ft. 4 in. and for the jump-off 4 ft. 4 in. only.

All these events are becoming every year more and more popular and, as expected, the participation and competition is stronger.

The 15 different movements for the Dressage part of the
COMBINED CAPRILI: SECOND DAY
(See Fig. 5).

1   Enter Ring in collected walk and stop at 1; salute the Judges.

2   1—3 Collected trot.

3   3—6 Extended trot and change direction from 6—2, changing
your diagonals in centre.

4   2—6 Collected trot.

5   6—7 Change direction by making half a volte.

6   7—8 Collected trot and change of direction by half a volte.

7   7—5 Collected walk and stop.

8   5 Advance 10 paces to centre, then back 6 paces, then right
angle to 4.

9   4—2 Walking on two tracks (Passage), the horse facing the
inside of R., then walk to 8.

10   8—6 Two tracking, the horse facing the outside at 30 degree
angle.

11   6—6 Collected canter LEFT LEAD, then full volte and stop,
then half-turn on the hindquarters until the horse faces
Judges.

12   6—6 Collected canter on right lead.

13   6—8 Collected trot and change of direction at 8 by inverted
half-volte.

14   8—1 Extended trot.

15   At 1, half-volte and stop, facing Judges, salute and complete
volte leave the ring in collected trot.

To be executed by memory. 10 points maximum per movement;
maximum total 150 points.

Three Judges in attendance. Average of the three scores to be taken
as final decision.

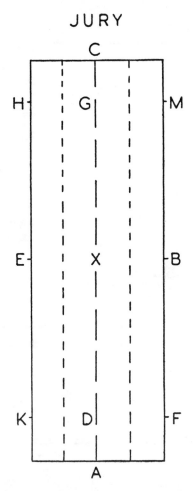

Fig. 3.—ARENA FOR DRESSAGE TESTS WITH OLD-FASHIONED
MARKINGS
Letters are used instead of the modern tests *Numbers*. The Arena is
60 metres × 20 metres

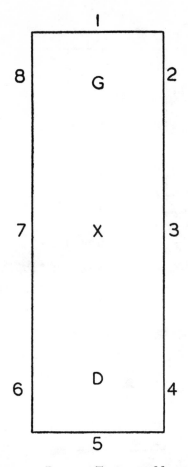

Fig. 4.—Arena for Dressage Tests with Modern Markings
Numbers have proved easier to memorise than letters, particularly
when the test consists of almost 50 movements.
Dimensions are the same: 60 × 20 metres.

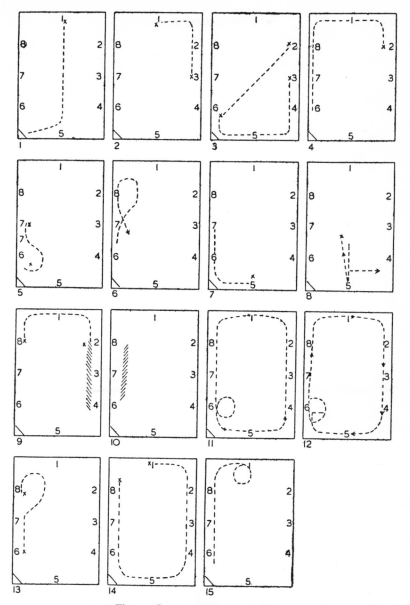

Fig. 5.—SIMPLIFIED DRESSAGE TEST:
Advisable when introduced in countries where Dressage was not
previously practised

EVENTS IN HORSE SHOWS NOT INCLUDED IN THE ONES RECOM-
MENDED BY THE F.E.I.:

Personally, I know nothing of the aims governing hack
classes and therefore am no authority on the matter, but I have
always thoroughly enjoyed watching these splendid horses
performing, even if the tests seemed to consist of rather elementary movements. In such a hack class in a British Dominion I
watched with mild curiosity a judge pick out three greys, try them
out one after another and then give them first, second and third
prizes, although there were several other horses in that same class
which were as good or as bad as the three greys. Always eager to
discover the finer points of judging hacks, and to satisfy my
curiosity, I asked the judge why he had picked out just those
three greys. He informed me with disarming candour that he
'liked greys'! 'The whole bunch of them were not good,' he
explained, then added, 'I happen to like greys, that's why I
picked them out.' However, his rather unorthodox method of
selection seemed to meet with the approval of both public and
competitors.

Being rightly or wrongly considered as a connoisseur of
horse-flesh, I was often invited to judge such events. To hide my
utter ignorance of the matter, I bore in mind the wise words of
the judge with a preference for greys and bravely stood my
ground. I let the horses ride round and round until I was dizzy,
then lined them up and simply picked out the three prettiest
girls! I have to admit that I, personally prefer beautiful blondes
to hefty greys! And exactly as in the case of the judge with the
preference for hefty greys, my Judgment of Paris act was popular
—even more popular than his.

There is something charming about the many English horse
shows, and really nothing in the world can compare with their
colourful atmosphere, enhanced by the beauty of the English
countryside. I admit I had a somewhat mistaken opinion of
English horse shows, but after I had had the privilege of assisting

at many of them in company with my old friend, Colonel Gibson, my opinion was completely reversed. The most pleasant part of my recent stay in England was spent assisting at all the country horse shows. I enjoyed every moment of those shows even though they were somewhat marred by an outbreak of foot-and-mouth disease. It was wonderful to watch the fine hackneys going through their paces and I enjoyed even more watching their miniature counterparts, the hackney ponies. In the United States I very much admired the five-gaited classes; horses of exceptional beauty with long, flowing manes and tails trailing to the ground. The American three-gaited classes correspond roughly to the English hack classes and are as pleasant to watch. Other interesting classes in the United States were the farmers' horse classes—five-gaited animals which were shown under the saddle, then inspanned and then even sent over a few obstacles.

In France I watched a special class of three-year-old Anglo-Arabs and Anglo-Normand horses shown under the saddle. Out of some 250 horses I truly could not pick out the winners. All I could do was eliminate two or three as not sufficiently good for that class, as I had previously done when watching the hunter classes in New York.

Ever since horsemen have taken part in jumping events, there has been a long and heated controversy over the number of obstacles used in a given event, their height, and the distances between those obstacles. As I have already mentioned, the modern show course originated from the English hunting field, when a few obstacles were scattered over the ground. Later, as this fascinating sport gained more adherents, the courses naturally were gradually changed, condensed and made more complicated every year. Whereas earlier only single jumps were used, double and, later on, triple jumps combined into one obstacle became popular and were used in almost every event with the exception of American events and puissance events. Now, although some horsemen and organisers maintained that the number of the combined jumps should be kept low, others advocated that the more combined obstacles were used, the more spectacular and, oddly enough, safer became the courses.

There are only two types of combined obstacles, i.e., groups of three jumps and groups of two jumps. A three-jump obstacle, for instance, might consist of (1) a brush, (2) post and rails, (3) a hog's back. The distances between the jumps in this group for a novice event at a speed of 330 yards per minute would be:

1 and 2	24 ft.
2 and 3	35 ft.

In a top category event, at a speed of 550 yards per minute, the jumps would be higher and would be spaced thus:

1 and 2	27 ft.
2 and 3	40 ft.

In a two-jump obstacle (for instance, a brush and then a wall) the difference in spacing would be:

Slow speed	23 ft.
Fast speed	27 ft.

An obstacle is never composed of more than three jumps; with more it becomes a jumping lane. Only in the six-bar event are six jumps considered as one.

We have, therefore, combined obstacles consisting of two or three jumps separated from each other by one stride and a jump or two strides and a jump.

One stride and jump—maximum	27 ft.
minimum	22 ft.
Two strides and jump—maximum	40 ft.
minimum	35 ft.

The distances must always be measured from the centre of a spread jump.

A horse's strides vary from 8 ft. to 20 ft. according to the speed at which it is travelling and therefore, as I have said before, the distances separating one group of obstacles from another are calculated on the speed at which the horse is supposed to be galloping.

The reader may use the following tables as a basis when trying out such courses.

Taking a novice event with a speed of 330 yards per minute the distances should be:

One stride and jump	22 ft.
Two strides and jump	35 ft.
Three strides and jump	47 ft.
Four strides and jump	59 ft.
Five strides and jump	71 ft.

The longer the distance between the jumps, the more easily can the length of the horse's strides be reduced from 12 ft. to 10 ft., because in an open stretch the rider can collect his horse a little and thus reduce the length of its strides by almost a foot. This is usually the case round turns in a course.

In a First Category event at a speed of 550 yards per minute, the distances should be as follows:

One stride and jump	27 ft.
Two strides and jump	40 ft.
Three strides and jump	53 ft.
Four strides and jump	66 ft.
Five strides and jump	80 ft.

The distances vary slightly because the first strides that a horse takes after coming down over a high jump are comparatively short, gradually stretching out and becoming longer as the horse gathers speed again.

There is another factor which had to be taken into consideration when erecting such courses, and that is the structure of the jumps. The distance between two vertical jumps, for instance, should be greater than that between a vertical and an inclined jump.

Let us take a novice course of 330 yards per minute and an obstacle of three jumps which must be constructed thus:

Jump No. 1   Brush
Jump No. 2   Post and rails
Jump No. 3   Triple bar

The distances between these jumps should be:

Between Jumps 1 and 2   24 ft.
Between Jumps 2 and 3   35 ft.

If the reader will take a piece of paper and draw this group of jumps in profile and then draw the line of the parabolas of the jumps he will observe that the horse's parabola over the triple bar is well over the required height although in comparison it is two feet nearer to the first distance.

In short, they allowed a couple of feet more for straight vertical jumps and applied shorter distances to triple bars, hogs' backs and Liverpools, these being inclined jumps.

Vertical jumps are—post and rails, gates, picket fences, rustic fences, walls, closed roads, oxers, double oxers and parallel bars.

Inclined jumps are—triple bars, hogs' backs and Liverpools.

Double oxers and parallel bars should be erected in this manner: the front poles must be at least 4 in. to 6 in. lower than the back poles and there must be a minimum of three poles in front and two poles at the back. The same applies to parallel bars.

As I have mentioned before, a horse's eyes focus quite differently from ours and it cannot judge correctly the depth of an oxer or a parallel bar jump if the front poles are kept at the same height as those at the back. This is a matter of the utmost importance to those who are responsible for erecting courses. There are more accidents over these two particular types of jumps than over all the other jumps combined, yet if they are erected correctly practically all these accidents can be eliminated. On the other hand, the easiest jump for the horse is the triple bar because it is plainly visible and the horse can size it up correctly.

The reader will often have seen horses coming far too close to the jump—when it happens to be an oxer or a parallel bar—hitting the first poles with their knees or even their chests, but easily clearing the back poles. This is because they cannot see the jump correctly. At the level of their eyes the parallel bars seem to them to be a post-and-rails jump and they jump it accordingly.

If, however, the front three bars—which should be thick ones and clearly visible—are placed six inches lower than the two at the back of the jump, the jump will seem formidable to the horse, and it will in consequence take greater pains to clear it.

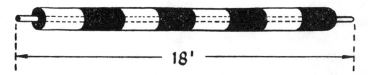

Fig. 6.—MAKING POLES

Old 2 in. water pipes covered thickly with sacking and stuffed with straw, then painted white with red, yellow, black or blue rings. This makes them clearly visible. Such soft poles will never hurt horses' legs. (*See also* fig. 7.)

As the reader will have followed, those courses were laid out in such a manner as to make the task of horse and rider as easy as possible. Although many horsemen today complain about too many combined obstacles, I am sure they would change their minds if they had had the opportunity of once negotiating such a well laid out course. I have found out they all complain about the excessive number of double and triple jumps for the simple reason that the distances between those jumps are now being deliberately ill-placed. I shall come to this later when describing actual courses. In those earlier courses every stride of the horse was calculated in advance! There was no reason whatsoever to PLACE one's horse, for that had already been done by the man who had laid out that course! I can truly state that those courses, although they seemed more formidable, were in fact quite safe.

All the rider had to do was get over the first jump and then just maintain his speed given for that course and he could negotiate every single following jump in his, or rather in his horse's, stride, without having to pull up or increase greatly the speed of his horse. In fact the horses cleared those courses with the same facility as a trained horse will clear a six-bar event, with the distances accurately measured between each jump.

Now, since this book was first written some nineteen years ago almost, the aims in show jumping have undergone quite a change. Whereas the earlier aim was to prepare and perfect more riders and HUSBAND the horses, by asking them to jump over more compact courses with accurately measured distances, the new tendency today is, unfortunately, clearly focused towards the spectacular and thrilling.

I shall not criticise here this new tendency, which rightly or wrongly has imposed itself and is now applied everywhere, for I am fully convinced that had it not been for this new tendency our passionate pursuit of show jumping would soon have faded out like so many other Victorian sports. Whereas we cared earlier about the opinion of a select few only, those who had dedicated themselves to this fine sport, the new tendency today is to act for the masses, for without the support of a large public, I have been assured that show jumping would have died.

It was again in France that this new tendency originated, indirectly helped again by the efforts of Colonel Cavaillé. As France was the only country to have over three hundred excellent show horses, mostly Anglo-Arabs then, in readiness, it naturally succeeded in swaying the majority of the Committee of the F.E.I. to its way of thinking.

As the motor has eliminated the ordinary horse, only those breeds of horses, serving a specific purpose, such as racing and show jumping, have a reasonable chance of survival. Now we all know that breeding horses is very expensive in Europe. The French, who have always had an excellent eye for good horse-flesh, moreover if benefits could be derived from that, soon

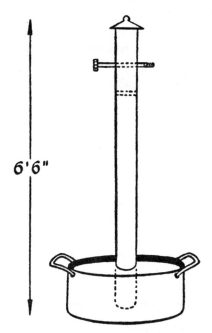

Fig. 7.—MAKING UPRIGHTS CHEAPLY

Again old water pipes, 4 to 5 in. in diameter and about 6 ft. 6 in. high. These pipes are embedded in a 4-gallon oil drum sawn in half and filled with cement. A few holes must be made in the bottom of the drum to allow water to run out. These uprights are very strong and will last a long time.

Holes are bored at 4-in. intervals to allow ordinary bolts, 8 in. long, to pass through. The ends of the bolts should be on the outside, to give a little support to the pole.

When painted in white and closed on top with a wooden cap, they look very good and always remain perfectly upright.

Handles are made by several wires pulled through two holes and twisted together.

In South American shows, where a great many jumps are used and courses are changed for every event, we use a small iron platform on two small wheels, with an iron bar attached to it. Thus we can simply push the uprights on the platform and pull them to whatever position is required.

began their selective breeding. (I am only writing about show jumpers now.) They very soon realised, and were the first, as a matter of fact, to do this, that producing a good show jumper was as selective a matter as producing fast race horses. They made a careful study of all their traditional breeds and came to the conclusion that they had to create an altogether new breed, specially adapted for jumping!

France's earlier breeders concentrated before mainly on three specific breeds:

(1) *The Anglo-Arab,* for the remounts of light cavalry.
(2) *The Anglo-Normand,* for the remounts of its heavy cavalry.
(3) *The Percheron,* the famous French heavy draught horse for all jobs.

I needn't mention here the other intermediary breeds as they are irrelevant to this book. They did not consider any one of these three breeds as ideally suited for show jumping and immediately went to task to create an altogether new breed, by selective breeding of the two first breeds and, I personally maintain, even of a few drops of Percheron blood into the bargain, so as to add weight and potency.

The result is what is known today as the 'Cheval de selle de France'—the French saddle horse! About the finest specimen of horse-flesh a man could wish to bestride!

Their earlier superiority in horses was soon enhanced by this new breed which proved its worth very soon. While the Germans were still trying to work out which of their many and excellent breeds was best suited to show jumping (Hannoveraner, Trakener or Holsteiner), the French just concentrated on their new breed and won most of the events. In England one cannot even find today a definite opinion as to which breed of horse is best suited for jumping. They seem to believe the same as I also did, that any sound, strong and well-built horse can make a good show jumper. That may be perfectly true, but if one now adds to those three primary conditions another one: QUALITY—or, as the

Frenchman calls it, CLASSE—all the better, and classe is what every French-bred horse has very much today.

Now the French are first and last sound business men. After thus producing their superb new horse breed they had to assure a market for it, and did. Courses were changed in French events so as to make it more and more difficult to negotiate them. The distances between the jumps were deliberately reduced or increased so as to make the horse almost an acrobat. The Puissance classes became more and more popular and, naturally, more spectacular. These new courses appealed far more to the eye of an outsider than the earlier smoother courses, well laid out and measured for the strides of the horses. I have seen courses laid out in such a way that in an important event NOT ONE horse managed to make a clear round. But the public simply howled with delight. The spectators who paid an entrance fee to see such events want first and last to see some action. They appreciate very little a smooth easy-seeming performance, but will vastly cherish a terrific struggle between horse and rider, and with spectacular falls added, may enjoy things even more.

The result of this new tendency is easily understood. The price of horses thus being capable of performing spectacular acrobatic feats rose steadily as more and more fine horses were senselessly being sacrificed to cater for thrills. Whereas we advocated earlier to husband our horses, to use and train them in a manner so that they should stay on their four legs as long as possible with us, the tendency now is to do the opposite! The French breeders must sell more and more fine horses to be able to keep up with the rising cost of breeding, and thus horses are used up and abused faster than ever to achieve just that. As I said, I am convinced that as matters are now the enthusiasm of the public would soon dwindle if we were to go back to our earlier aims. To make horse shows more appetising even for the paying public, betting booths have been set up at all Spanish show events and are doing a roaring business, just as at any ordinary race track.

Whereas before the war we used to pay around £150 to £300 for a first-class horse for jumping, a first-class horse today can cost anything up to £10,000 and in some cases even more!

Moreover, these new courses are all judged by the chronometer, that is speed. To win, a rider practically has to race the course over the single jumps, then he must pull up violently in front of a combined obstacle and try as best he can to struggle over. The reader can easily understand how far this 'teasing' can be carried out by deliberately making the distances impossible.

However, times change and we must march in step with progress. If the aims behind our fascinating sport have changed, the spirit is still there though and better and stronger horses are bred and ever better riders appear every year since those new methods are being applied.

Since the beginning of show jumping, there has existed the problem of judging such events. Many ways have been tried out, more or less satisfactorily. I cannot enumerate them all here, as I did in the earlier edition; suffice it to state that the F.E.I. has finally gained the upper hand and that there are only THREE officially recognised ways of judging—*Bareme A, B and C.*

(1) *Bareme A*

Simply by speed. The horse with the fastest time and least faults is the winner. The rest of this Bareme are too well known to enumerate them again. I only wish to express my personal opinion over the idiosyncracy of one of its rules—faults for refusal. Why should a horse which jumps spiritedly and just brushes a little against a pole, making it topple over, be penalised by four faults, while another horse which simply refuses to jump at all and stops dead like a mule in front of a jump is only penalised with three points? It simply does not make any sense. Before the war it was in reverse and far more logical, I feel. A refusal was then penalised by five faults, the second one by ten and not as now three and six faults only.

In my opinion the *Bareme A* has a great drawback. Let us say two horses have made clear rounds in an event where a jump-off (Barrage) is stipulated. The first of these two horses races over the course so as to win by time (over the reduced course of the jump-off) and he knocks down two jumps, hence eight faults, but in a very fast time.

Now the second rider canters as slowly as he can to avoid making faults and makes a clear round and wins, of course, although he may have taken over twenty-eight seconds MORE than the maximum time allowed! As time is counted as a quarter fault for each second over the maximum time allowed! This may seem very logical to the gentlemen of the F.E.I. but to me it is a Chinese puzzle.

(2) Bareme B

Only applied to courses under 700 yd. and is seldom used, same as *Bareme C* which is, if possible, even more complicated. The reader can find the details of these two mysterious ways of judging in the booklet issued by the F.E.I. I must warn the reader that he will gain little if any benefit from that lecture, which is about as incomprehensible as any official document could possibly be.

LIST OF WINNING TEAMS AND THE INDIVIDUAL GOLD MEDALS IN THE OLYMPIC GAMES

Fifth Olympiade of Stockholm 1912: Winning team Sweden.
Individual winner Captain Cariou, France, on Mignon.
Seventh Olympiade of Brussels in 1920: Winning team Sweden.
Individual winner Lieutenant Lequio, Italy.
Eighth Olympiade of Paris in 1924: Winning team Sweden.
Individual winner Lieutenant Gemuseus, Switzerland.
Ninth Olympiade of Amsterdam in 1928: Winning team Spain.
Individual winner Captain Ventura, Czechoslovakia.
Tenth Olympiade of Los Angeles in 1932: Only individual winner

Lieutenant Nishi, Japan. No team was classified as all were eliminated.

Eleventh Olympiade of Berlin in 1936: Winning team Germany. Individual winner Lieutenant Hasse on Tora, Germany.

Fourteenth Olympiade of London in 1948: Winning team Mexico. Individual winner Colonel Mariles on Arete, Mexico.

Fifteenth Olympiade of Helsinki in 1952: Winning team England. Individual winner D'Oriola on Ali-Baba, France.

Sixteenth Olympiade of Stockholm in 1956: Winning team Germany. Individual winner H. G. Winkler on Halla, Germany.

Seventeenth Olympiade of Roma in 1960: Winning team Germany. Individual winner Captain Raimundo d'Inzeo of Italy on Possilipo.

Eighteenth Olympiade of Tokio in 1964: Winning team Germany. Individual winner D'Oriola of France.

Nineteenth Olympiade of Mexico in 1968: Winning team Canada. Individual winner W. Steinkraus of United States.

LIST OF WORLD RECORDS IN HIGH JUMPING AND BROAD JUMPS

High Jump Records	metres
1900 Captain Crousse of France on Conspirateur	2.35
1912 M. Rene Ricard and M. Montespieu on Biskra and Montiole, tied at a height of	2.36
1933 Lieutenant de Castries of France on Vol-au-Vent	2.38
1938 Captain Gutiérrez of Italy on Osopo in Roma	2.44
1949 Captain Laraguibel on Huaso of Chile in Santiago (this is the world high jump record today)	2.49

Broad Jump Record of the World	
1912 M. Henri de Roeyr on Pick-me-up of France in Le Touquet	7.50
1913 M. Henri de Roeyr on Pick-me-up won again in Le Touquet—same distance	

1935 Lieutenant de Castries on Tenace of France in Spa   7.50
1946 Mr. J. Fraga-Patrao of Argentine, Buenos Aires,
      on Guarana   7.70
1948 Commander Nogueras on Balcamo and Captain
      Maestre on Salinas, both of Spain, establish a
      new record in Bilbao   8.00
1949 Mr. Van der Woort of Holland on Cœur Joli in
      The Hague   8.10
1950 Lieutenant-Colonel Nogueras on Balcamo of
      Spain in Bilbao   8.20
1951 Lieutenant-Colonel Lopez de Hierro on Amado
      Mio of Spain in Barcelona established the present
      world's record   8.30

Chapter Four

Saddlery and Gear

Riding is without doubt the most difficult of all sports for the simple reason that *two* thoroughly opposed personalities are involved, the rider and the horse. To achieve a desired result these two opposed personalities, with completely different temperaments and characters must collaborate 100 per cent, I fully realised this first when coaching eager horsemen in my modern methods, when they all invariably complained that they simply could not ride in a correct modern seat and sit in such a position when jumping. I very soon discovered that they were right and also the reason of their complaint—the saddle. I then naturally concentrated exhaustively on the saddle and to my amazement discovered that there were two villains who apparently had combined their efforts to make the practice of our beloved sport sheer misery: *The Saddler and the Tree-Maker!* But what also struck me as truly odd was the fact that not one rider in almost fifty years of show jumping had done more than just recognise this unsatisfactory state of affairs. But saddler and tree-maker were gentlemen, I soon discovered, who *never* rode themselves but had, for the entire century in which riding became a sport, been forcing riders to use their altogether inadequate contraptions!

With all other sports the player has only to choose the right implements and indulge in the sport of his choice. The golfer for instance before purchasing his clubs will take into account their weight and length and the angle of the head. The same is the case with the tennis player who must choose a racket which feels balanced. But for the rider this is not half the story. He has first to overcome the more or less rebellious nature of his horse then train his horse so that it will collaborate with him. That makes already two vitally important considerations. But then when the selection of equipment should have been a straightforward task, it was deeply shocking for me to realise that the saddler and the tree-maker were manufacturing totally inadequate products. They were not even collaborating. Thus our favourite sport depended on *four* independent factors, two of them, and the most important ones, beyond our control. True, one *could* ride out for a pleasant walk on such contraptions but they proved woefully inadequate for modern show jumping. When I was riding in big international events I always had to compete with equally good riders on equally good horses and carrying a handicap of over 30 lb. due to my height and weight. This and the pupil's complaints soon made me focus my attention on this all important fact, the *saddle*. I very soon discovered that for the horse to give its maximum performance it needed a maximum freedom of movement, and for the rider to give his mount this freedom he needed a saddle built in such a manner that it afforded him freedom of movement and seat. I soon appreciated the vicious circle that existed: if the rider was not comfortable on his saddle his horse was anything but comfortable under the rider and so on. I therefore began collecting saddles from all over the world and very soon had a most interesting collection which I then studied thoroughly one by one noting their merits and defects. I soon discovered then that the most comfortable saddles and at the same time the safest ones were the saddles used in countries where a man still worked with his horse or used it as a current means of transportation: these were the countries such as Turkey, Persia, the Mongol countries and Arab lands, southern Spain and most of the South American countries. All the saddles from those countries showed almost identical characteristics: they were short and very deep in the seat, thus exactly the opposite of the then universally adopted and so-called English saddle! What the horseman of those 'horse' countries apparently most sought after was the sensation of sitting *in* the saddle and never *on* the saddle! True, all those saddles I collected showed also the same defect, a defect only as far as our modern sport of show jumping was concerned: they sat too high upon the horse's back! But there again it was for a very sound reason: the Eastern horseman, exactly as his counterpart, the Spanish or Chilean Vaquero, needed a free area of action *over* his horse's head, be it for fighting or or swinging the 'lasso' to catch a steer—unnecessary for a jumping event. I thus concentrated upon one very important factor—how to build a saddle that would have all the advantages of the Eastern saddle but at the same time be as near the horse's back as possible. This was of the utmost importance, for we all know that the higher the point of gravity is placed the less is the stability. I daresay, though, that any one of my saddles from Eastern countries would be far more comfor-table for jumping than most of the old-fashioned English-style saddles which have now pretty well disappeared, or some of the French and German saddles. But I do not mean by this that riders should use a Persian ceremonial saddle or an Andalusian Vaquero saddle for show jumping.

After gathering all these facts I went to see my own saddler and complained that his best saddles were not good enough for modern show events. That worthy man almost threw a fit and indignantly explained that he was the seventh generation of saddle makers. I soothed him as well as I could and invited him to select the best jumping saddle in his shop, a thing which he did rather proudly. I then drove with him to my riding club, strapped his contraption on to one of my best show jumpers, erected a course of some fourteen obstacles with an average height of five feet and invited him very politely to try out himself his masterpiece over that course! He stared at me open-mouthed, then at the high obstacles and the impatient horse, then did something odd. He sat on the ground, scratching his head and mumbled crestfallen: 'By God, sir, I have never been on a horse in my life and neither have I ever put my bottom on one of my saddles, now that I come to think of it.' And this was the grand old master of saddlery, seventh generation of saddle makers on whose contraptions we, the riders had to risk our bones over difficult courses! After he recovered from his initial trauma, he visibly brightened and eagerly announced that he was not the man to be blamed, but that the real villain was the *tree-maker*! So I discovered the second miscreant in this sinister plot to ruin all pleasure in our sport! When we got to the tree-maker and my saddler pointed him out as the *true* villain, the tree-maker almost hit him with one of his choice trees and for sure would have caused the poor chap grievous bodily harm without my prompt intervention! When their tempers had cooled somewhat I got them to sit down and talk the problem over calmly. I explained to them what the rider's problems were: where it hurt the rider, where the saddle or tree was too broad or too shallow etc. and after some hours of discussions we finally drew some new model trees and built saddles on them, which I tried out with the most demanding tests. After building some 40 to 50 saddles and taking them to pieces again, we finally created what has since been accepted as a near-perfect jumping saddle.

I admit that at first it was most difficult to make the riders see my point when I introduced this new saddle. Practically all insisted that any old saddle was good enough for a good rider and that a good rider did not need such a 'sissy' contraption to win an event! This attitude was naturally too stupid to bother with but once they *did* sit on this modern saddle those same tough riders immediately agreed that 'I had something there' and very soon adopted the saddle, though they objected to the price! I had to point out to them the obvious paradox of their erroneous viewpoint. I asked them calmly how much they had paid for their champion horse. Some had paid as much as £3,000 to £4,000 for their mounts! (This, by the way, is not an exceptionally high price nowadays, extraordinary as it may seem. I have witnessed in Spain, not exactly the wealthiest country in Europe, a horse being bought for 3,500,000 pesetas, or roughly 50,000 dollars!)

After that it was easy to make them understand the absurdity of their point—it amounted virtually to buying a Rolls-Royce car and for the sake of economy fitting it with second-hand re-tread tyres! It was quite another matter though to overcome the patriotic feelings of the valiant British, German and French riders. Quite rightly the British horsemen considered their country as *the* country of perfection for anything connected with horse and saddlery. They proudly pointed out to me that people would come from every country in the world to England to buy their riding outfits, breeches, boots, saddlery and all, and that in short, the British were fully convinced that they and *they* only had virtually invented the horse and riding.

Oddly enough the even more patriotic Frenchmen also insisted that they and not the 'merchant' Englishmen had invented the horse, riding and anything connected with it. The stolid Germans protested, vehemently almost, insisting that horse and saddle were a well-known Teutonic invention as every child in Germany knew, and had been invented as far back as the good old days of their Teutonic Military order of Königsberg. In short, a lot of inventors. Pity that none of those patriotic gentlemen ever thought of taking patent rights on the horse as we would have witnessed some quite amusing court cases.

But oddly enough all the European horse-inventors seemed to overlook the insignificant fact that old Genghis Khan, of evil memory, also insisted in his days that he had invented horse and harness and virtually proved *his* case when his fabulous swordsmen almost conquered the entire known world. And before Old Genghis, the Huns, the Avares, the Parthes and other Asiatic horse people would have held the same view. Even young Alexander, the Macedon, is supposed to have had a pretty good cavalry and could boast in his days, quite rightly, that he did in fact invent at least part of the horse, the horse-shoe, For it was during his crossing over the Khyber Pass that the horse-shoe was invented, if not by the great conqueror himself, at least by his men. An even earlier horse inventor was the resourceful Greek, Xenophon, who, by the way, wrote the first book about horses and riding. But he, of course, disdained both saddle and breeches!

'THE ENGLISH SADDLE'

When I returned to England again, 12 years after having introduced there my modern saddle, I had the pleasant satisfaction of seeing that my saddle was used and manufactured extensively and had encouraged the production of others employing many of the principles upon which mine had been made! That famous old English saddle had largely disappeared, at least as far as competition riding was concerned.

I know it is slightly boastful, but I do now believe that the modern saddle I introduced to England, and which served as a pattern for many others, was partly instrumental in the great equestrian post-war successes of the British teams in international jumping events, and so were the modern methods as expounded in this book. Some patriotic English readers will still sternly refute this but I would point out that before the war the British teams were only 'brilliant in their absence' amongst the international jumping events on the Continent. In fairness it has to be said that pre-war British riding cannot really be compared with the situation that exists today, when the scope of riding in Britain has been so much extended and the emphasis has tended to move away from the hunting field and towards active competition. Nonetheless, it is a fact that since the war, or at any rate since the early fifties, when my saddle was introduced and this book ap-appeared in its first edition, the British teams have regularly appeared amongst the winners of international events and must now be regarded as a strong force in jumping at these levels. I would not claim that my saddle and this book were responsible for this happening but I feel that they may have given an added impetus to the successful entry of the British into international riding.

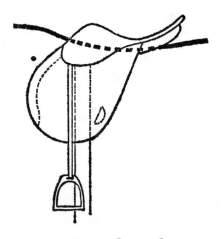

Fig. 8.—MODERN JUMPING SADDLE

This gives the rider the impression of being seated *in* the horse rather than *on* the horse. It is necessary that the stirrup bar should be placed further forward than in a normal saddle, to position the rider correspondingly, and to allow his legs, by placement of the girth straps forward, to be in close contact with his horse.

A correct modern jumping saddle must have these indispensible characteristics, without which it would be absolutely useless for jumping:

(1) It must be made of very soft leather so that the rider is completely comfortable on it right from the first day he uses it.

(2) The seat must be as deep and short as possible. The short-ness of the seat is far more important than many riders seem to realise, for too long a seat induces the rider to shift his weight at the moment of jumping which is

about the worst thing a rider can do to his struggling horse.

(3) The tree must be fitted with steel springs so as to prevent the rider's weight from shifting backwards upon the horse's most sensitive part, its kidneys, should he be left behind over a fence. This spring tree, because of its resilience, also affords greater comfort to the rider and, most importantly, to the horse, since it will 'give' to the movements made by the back, a property not found in a tree of the 'rigid' variety (i.e. one made without the longitudinal strips of sprung steel laid from front to rear). Additionally, a rigid tree cannot be expected to give the rider that feeling of being really close to his horse and most limit the effectiveness of contact between the rider's seat and the horse's back.

(4) The saddle must be as narrow as possible between the thighs of the rider so as not to spread them apart and should allow practically the whole length of the rider's legs to be in contact with his horse.

(5) The saddle must be so constructed as to have barely the thickness of soft leather between the rider's legs and the horse's body so that the rider can *feel* his horse's muscles working between his legs.

(6) The saddle must have a high knee support, not to help the rider's knees, which if he sits correctly he will practically never use, but only to keep the rider's leg in exactly the correct position and hence his whole body (this is where it interferes the least with his horse's freedom of movement). The other reason for this high knee support is to prevent the rider from sliding forwards *after* the jump when the horse is already landing. Lastly, the modern saddle must be light, around 10 lb., but without loss in strength.

Modern jumping saddles of this type have now been available in England for almost 16 years and I shall not enlarge further on the design but it may be of interest to the English reader to discuss briefly, the French and German saddles.

THE FRENCH SADDLE

Many of the French saddles, are derived from the Danloux saddle and some of them are about the worst I have ever come across in all European countries! Colonel Danloux was a first-class French cavalry officer who in his time already had realised the short-comings of the French saddles and had tried to make some sensible changes. I have seen original models of the saddle devised by Colonel Danloux but I daresay that that excellent officer and very successful rider would turn in his grave were he to see some of the examples which have since been termed 'Danloux' saddles.

The worst of the French saddles have every single defect of all the other saddles made in Europe in earlier days and *none* of their very few good qualities! This may sound to be a very harsh criticism but I shall explain:

(1) They are terribly heavy, weighing around 25 lb.

(2) The leather used, although of excellent grain and colour, is very thick and stiff. It is similar in consistency to the leather used in the old-fashioned English saddle.

(3) The saddles are extremely broad between the legs often up to 10 in. wide across the waist when compared with the 4 in. of the Toptani saddle. Thus the rider's thighs are spread enormously and hence his whole leg position goes to pieces.

(4) The bridge, or front arch, is far too weak and shows a tendency to spread open after a couple of months use with most unfortunate results. The rider is then obliged to sit too far forward with his whole weight on the horse's forelegs. To negotiate a jump on such a saddle the rider's weight must necessarily, be thrown even more forward, often with the head being held lower than the buttocks, thus handicapping greatly the unfortunate horse.

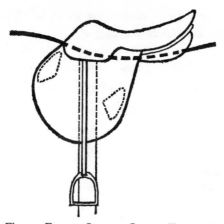

Fig. 9.—FRENCH SADDLE, CALLED 'DANLOUX'
The rider is seated too high on the horse because of the excessive padding of the panel, and the faulty construction of the seat. The tree itself is so broad as to spread the rider's thighs, thus reducing effective contact by his legs.

(5) The panels are stuffed far too full, particularly at the cantle. The result is that the rider is raised away from the horse's back and denied the essential contact between his seat and the horse. What is more it raises the rider's point of gravity to an unacceptable degree, as well as tipping him forward should the cantle-end of the panel be stuffed over-generously.

A contributory reason for this abnormality is the fact that should the front arch spread the saddle sits too low in front and becomes out of balance. To counteract this defect a thick pad or a felt namna is used to correct the deficiency. But then this has the effect of making the saddle too low at the rear and so back it goes to the saddler to have more stuffing inserted. And so it goes on until the famous Danloux saddle resembles that of an Andalusian Vaquero, without being as comfortable.

I pointed this out to Colonel Cavaillé when he was training the French team at Fontainebleau many years ago and though some of the French saddlers could not be persuaded to see the point improvements have been made and some of the more glaring errors in construction eradicated.

There are now French saddles made on the lines of the original Toptani but many of the French top riders use modern saddles made in countries other than their own.

THE GERMAN SADDLE

Similarly, the old type German saddle was an absolute miscarriage if I may use this expression as I think it suits it best. I shall explain: The old-fashioned German saddle was exactly like its English cousin—a long, shallow contraption, derived from the old German cavalry saddle. The leather used was, if possible, even thicker and stiffer than the leather used for the English saddle. I suppose this was due to the now incomprehensible view that a saddle must survive at least 10 horses. This was the rule in the old cavalry regiments. Or, perhaps it was the idea that the sons and grandsons of the brave German horsemen should suffer for the sins of their elders!

Perhaps German horsemen were particularly heavy and believed that a heavy man needed a heavy saddle, when exactly the opposite is true.

Initially, the German saddle-makers overlooked many of the qualities inherent in my modern saddle, although they did deepen the seat and shorten it as well as begin to make use of a resilient tree.

The present-day German saddle still does not incorporate all the design points of the Toptani; the tree, for instance, is usually made with a quarter cut-back head, but it is far narrower in the waist than ever before, soft, light leather is used and it is not nearly so heavy.

Indeed, saddles by Stubben, Kieffer and Passier, as well as by other German makers, enjoy considerable popularity outside Germany, particularly, in the U.S.A., where they are imported in some quantity.

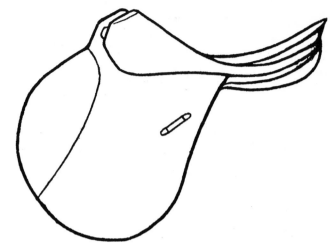

Fig. 10—MODERN GERMAN SADDLE

Some of them, however, still retain a dressage look about them and are not entirely suitable for jumping.

Surprisingly, the Germans, a conservative people, have a strong inclination towards fancy innovations and some of their products are so decorative that they look almost like a German version of the fancy Mexican parade saddles. But, perhaps, that is the influence of the American market.

The consequences of using the old type of German saddle for jumping were simply appalling. One saw hundreds of valiant German riders indulging in the most extraordinary acrobatics. They would approach the obstacle at a very slow canter and when a few strides away would lean back and make peculiar rotating movements with the hindquarters firmly fixed to the saddle. Then, suddenly, the weight would be thrust forward over the horse's neck and the rest left to chance. When asked why they behaved in this fashion I got the most baffling answer, 'Herr So and So', one of the most successful German show riders, 'did it this way and he always won!'

Today's German riders win a lot of international events, specialising in their own particular brand of precision jumping, which is admittedly very effective on occasions.

But then, the British and French do a lot of winning, too, and I am not entirely convinced that either German saddles or the style of riding employed is entirely helpful to the German exponents of the sport of show jumping.

In my view much of their success is due to the outstanding quality of the superb German horses, which are admittedly supremely well-schooled in the German method. In my humble opinion these horses are the finest types in the world for jumping. I am sure, though, that all European show riders will sooner or later switch to the Thoroughbred, as the Americans have done to a large degree. But even then I am convinced that the German breeders will produce bigger and better Thoroughbred jumpers.

THE ITALIAN SADDLE

As I mentioned earlier it was due to the two genial Italian masters, Frederico Caprili and his disciple, Piero Santini, that modern horsemanship of the sort practised today was introduced. As a matter of fact, until these two came on the scene horsemanship was very much concerned with indoor riding, based on the schooling of the horse which had flowered in the Renaissance period and had been later brought to refinement by De la Guérin- ière. Oddly enough much of it went back to Xenophon (430– 350 BC), the first cavalry general to introduce a system of cavalry training and to write about it.

In the last century European riding, outside England, was dominated by the existing cavalry schools and few people rode for pleasure. It was Caprili's revolutionary methods which changed cavalry training which, up to that point, had been concentrated to a great extent on balance and collection imposed within the confines of the indoor school and with little regard for its relevance in the field of action. Caprili overthrew the old taboos and changed completely the seat and methods of training, especially as they concerned jumping. By doing so he opened the way to the delightful sport we enjoy today.

It was quite quickly realised, however, that these new methods could not be taught without adequate saddles and a modern saddle was produced with the help of an open-minded Italian saddler, Pariani of Milan. Thus was born the Pariani saddle, the first to employ a spring tree, incidentally, and the forerunner of today's saddles.

With its help the Italian teams have, ever since, been amongst the leaders in international competition. The reader should bear in mind that even now only a couple of thousand men and women practise riding, let alone jumping, in all Italy. There are hundreds of times this number in England, Germany, and France. I believe that this argues very much in favour of the Pariani, which for 50 years has been a well-known name in the equestrian world.

Although the Pariani changed and was improved over the years (Santini, in fact, gave his name to a saddle made on a 'parchment' tree which was manufactured in England during the early 1930s and which was based on the Pariani model) the sport of jumping itself underwent an even greater change. By the 1950s a new saddle was needed and that was when the Toptani came into being.

Today's Italian saddles, much improved upon when compared with the early models, have drawn something, I think, from the design features of the Toptani.

The reader will appreciate, however, what tremendous opposition I had to overcome when introducing another saddle with a 'Dago' name into England of all countries.

Although the excellent Pariani had existed for half a century it was only used by a comparatively small number of riders and it could hardly be said to have gained even a footing in traditionalist

England, although one or two similar saddles were manufactured there.

The Toptani, however, within two years of the first one being made in England, virtually eliminated the conventional hunting saddle in competitive sport. It was tantamount to going to the Lowenbrau in Munich and telling them their beer was lousy and that they would do better to buy Spanish beer instead.

A well-constructed saddle is already half the battle won for the show rider. I have proved that almost 90 per cent of all faults committed can be avoided with a good saddle; also 90 per cent of all accidents. If the rider is not comfortable on his saddle he must seek instinctively an extra support, the nearest being the reins, and thus his horse's mouth. If he hangs on to the horse's mouth he throws it off balance and shortens the horse's vision. Again, it's all a vicious circle. A good saddle should allow the rider to sit firmly, not needing his hands for anything other than guiding his horse. He ought to be able to jump with his hands a foot lower than the withers and at least 6 in. away from both sides of the horse's neck, thus giving it perfect freedom of the mouth and full balance of its neck. Whenever saddles are the subject of discussion I hear the same odd argument, 'Yes, but English saddles are the best because they last longest!' I have never disputed the excellent workmanship of English saddlers; it is the very finest in the world. Friends of mine have shown me saddles made by famous English saddlers which in some cases had been in use for three generations, they told me with pride. It never seemed to occur to them that it was rather foolish to use such old-fashioned sports gear, although they would not have dreamt of using their grandfather's penny-farthing bicycle or their father's 1909 motor car. So why they insisted on using their grandfather's saddles I cannot understand, unless it was a form of penance. I have many saddles in my collection, some of which have been in my family since the seventeenth century, and which are still in excellent condition. I should, however, feel very self-conscious,

Haute Ecole—Dressage
Cadre Noir Saumur

DIFFERENCE IN TRAINING METHODS

Results of using the placing jump (not visible here but 45 ft. away) for restraining a horse prone to get *under* the jump. By this modern method the horse, which used only to cat-jump, was trained to 'stand back' and negotiate broad jumps

SADDLE AND GEAR

MODERN JUMPING SADDLES (*above and below*)

(1) Exceptionally deep seat.

(2) Forward set stirrup bars which keep the rider's weight in the correct place.

(3) Shape moulded to the horse, allowing the rider to sit practically on the horse's back.

(4) Well-padded knee rolls under the flaps, which keep the rider in position and give him strong support.

(5) (*below*) Inlaid stirrup bars which eliminate the annoying bulk caused by the leathers and buckle.

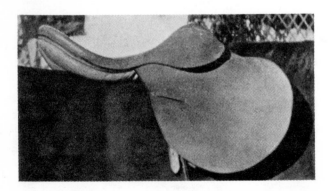

and no doubt look very silly, if I entered a modern show ring riding on a splendid Persian ceremonial saddle, although it would be far more comfortable than the average English saddle. My advice is: hang your old saddles on the walls of your home as antiques—they might serve as a substitute for etchings.

THE CORRECT BIT AND THE DROP NOSEBAND

The indicated bit for a show jumper is the snaffle with a drop noseband. Personally, I prefer a soft flexible rubber snaffle to an ordinary one. I have found that horses with cast-iron mouths are more easily handled with a rubber snaffle.

After the Berlin Olympic Games I interviewed several German cavalry instructors and all of them attributed the extraordinary success of the German riders to (*a*) hard work, (*b*) correctly measured courses, and (*c*) the drop noseband. This may surprise the reader, but actually the drop noseband is as important in show jumping as the forward seat saddle. It gives you all the collection you need and, at the same time, is easy on the horse's mouth. Its function is simple; it prevents the horse from opening its mouth and in consequence losing a few lengths round a sharp turn. When the horse tries to open its mouth it collects itself by pulling its own nose down. Lastly, it prevents the horse from leaning on the bit.

The Duke of Newcastle, that great horseman and connoisseur, used it as long ago as the seventeenth century, and gives a colourful description of it in his famous book on dressage. Like many other excellent English ideas which have fallen into disuse in England, it was picked up by foreigners, who have used it successfully ever since.

A useful innovation has recently been produced in French show-jumping circles. The invention of a young horseman, Jacques Bessin, this is a bridle based on the hackamore and achieves control without the usual collection of iron operating upon the mouth.

The Bessin bridle operates upon both upper and lower jaws by a system of levers that enable the rider to position his horse's head to the best possible advantage, obtaining maximum control whilst imposing the very minimum of discomfort on a strong, galloping horse operating within the confines of the jumping arena.

The degree of success achieved by this bridle, on a variety of horses, is quite remarkable. M. Bessin's invention could well be the answer to the problem of the strong horse who loses precious seconds at the turns and twists inherent in modern jumping courses.

THE DUMB JOCKEY

Every reader will probably have seen one of these contrivances. It is a large surcingle with two horns on it, through which run rubber reins to the bit. The whole thing is strapped to the horse and connected to the tail by a crupper. The reins are shortened and when harnessed with this contraption the horse will have the appearance of being collected. Its head will be low, its neck arched, its back shortened and its tail up. Leaving his horse to stand like this in its box for a couple of hours at a time, the trainer would sit down to smoke his pipe at leisure.

What he forgot, of course, was that a spirited horse is naturally collected without a rider on its back. It needs only dressage and collection to counteract the effect of a rider's weight. Therefore, although the dumb jockey was an ingenious idea and quite efficacious in the training of young colts when lunging them, the moment it was removed and the horse mounted by a rider the collection was gone. Nothing has yet been invented to replace the rider's legs; without using your legs for an hour every day you can never collect your horse.

THE STANDING MARTINGALE

Of all the short cuts used in training a horse this is undoubtedly the worst. It is a clear proof that the rider's seat is radically wrong, and that he lacks any knowledge of elementary dressage. If, instead of using all sorts of gadgets and short cuts, the rider would only take his horse into the manège and work it correctly for a couple of hours every day, he would not need to employ this extraordinary device.

It was invented originally to counteract the effect of the rider's seat. If you sit on a horse with all your weight on the horse's loins, and your feet well forward, you are already out of balance and have to hang on to the horse's mouth every time it makes a sudden movement, because you haven't really got a seat at all and, therefore, no grip. The horse then becomes hollow-backed because it has not been trained to develop the new seats of muscles which it requires to carry a rider's weight. Directly the horse's back becomes hollow up goes its head, and whenever the rider hangs on to the horse's mouth—as he is obliged to do—the head goes higher, until the horse becomes a stargazer and is useless for jumping.

This is where the standing martingale comes in. Instead of taking the horse into the manège, sitting on it correctly, giving it continual leg pressure and holding the reins firmly every time it tries to jerk its head—all of which would get the horse's head down quite easily—a lazy rider straps it down with a standing martingale.

To my mind the moment a horse needs a standing martingale to get its nose down it no longer has any business in a show ring. It should either be in the manège or in a vegetable cart! A horse which throws its head up does so only because the rider is sitting incorrectly. In any case, a horse which has been ridden for some time on a standing martingale and still throws it head up is generally useless for jumping because it cannot look at the jumps if its nose is higher than its eyes. Such a horse is a danger to itself and to its rider. Unfortunately, I have seen in earlier shows hundreds of such horses with this dreadful contrivance strapped to them. I have seen something even worse: a standing martingale attached very tightly to a drop noseband. This to my mind is not only stupid but criminal, and yet I knew one riding master who used it on all his horses and taught his pupils to do the same. A horse's most sensitive part is his nose, where the bone is soft. The reader can imagine, therefore, how the poor animal suffers when it tries to stretch out its neck in order to jump and finds it strapped to its belly. Moreover, if the horse needs a standing martingale it is entirely your fault and the horse is being penalised for your mistakes. My advice is: if the horse is not entirely ruined, take this terrible contraption off and throw it away; take your horse back into the manège and start working it properly by sitting correctly and using your legs as they should be used.

Even in hack shows, where you can sit your horse as you like, the use of a standing martingale is not allowed. How much more wrong, then, it is to use the martingale in a jumping class where you must have a correct seat and where the horse must have absolute freedom of its neck and mouth to be able to jump.

The whole thing is a vicious circle. If you sit wrongly the horse will throw its head up. If the horse throws its head up it cannot see the jump properly and cannot jump properly; you have to try to place it into the jump. If you are concentrating on placing the horse you cannot keep a correct seat. If you cannot keep a correct seat your horse throws its head up—and so it goes on. Therefore be sensible: throw away this idiotic gadget; learn to ride correctly and then train your horse correctly.

Moreover the standing martingale is only a leftover of the old cavalry equipment. It was then necessary to keep the horse's head low so that the trooper could wield his sword or lance in cavalry battles but it is certainly *not* necessary for show jumping! However, with the increased knowledge of methods of training I am glad to note that the standing martingale is now banned in most areas of jumping and not seen to any great degree elsewhere.

SIDE REINS

These form another frightful contrivance. They may be all right for a heavy, slow circus horse, which only canters slowly round in a circle on a perfectly clear track, but for ordinary equitation they are are quite useless and extremely dangerous. I have seen them used many times, unfortunately. What they actually do is to give the horses cast-iron mouths; they never improve them.

The reason for this is that a horse cannot keep its neck continually arched, and tends to rest its head by leaning on the bit, thus developing an almost insensitive mouth on top of a hard one.

For ordinary riding and training in a manège this device may possibly be permissible, but it is criminally stupid and unforgivable to use it on a hunter or a show jumper. A horse cannot jump when trussed up like a chicken, any more than an athlete could jump if his arms were strapped behind his back. I have seen many poor animals break their jaws and sometimes their necks in this manner, because the first thing a horse does when it loses its balance is stretch out its neck and it cannot do this if the bit is strapped firmly to the saddle girth by strong leather reins.

Once more I have to revert to the dangerous tendency for quick results, which forces riders to use cruel short cuts. If a horse has developed a so-called hard mouth it is always due to the bad training and ignorant handling it has received. No horse is ever born with a hard mouth, but many riders unfortunately have to rely on their hands to keep them in an already precarious seat and so they drag on the horse's mouth. When a horse finally develops a hard mouth there is no point in 'over-bitting' it. If it is worth retraining take all the ironmongery out of its mouth and start again from the beginning, using only a soft rubber snaffle and drop noseband or a hackamore. After a few months of patient training the horse will develop a normal mouth and can then be gradually bitted up to a snaffle and drop noseband, and a bit and bridoon for ordinary equitation and dressage.

BLINKERS

I shall waste no time enlarging on this contrivance. It may be necessary for a young carthorse in dense city traffic; it may even be necessary for a timid racehorse which is afraid of being crowded in a race, but it has no place whatever in a show ring, where the horse has the whole arena to itself. If you see someone using it in jumping you may safely assume that that horse has been ill-treated to such an extent that it is afraid to get near a jump as it probably expects to find there a man armed with a long steel rod to hit it over the forelegs and belly—in short, to rap it.

A well-trained horse does not need rapping. You can never use pain as a means of training, if you want your horse to remain on its legs and become a good jumper. It is impossible to over-emphasise this point.

If you want to enjoy riding and jumping it is essential to remember the following points:

Never rush the training of your horse.

Never brutalise your horse.

Never try to teach your horse something you don't know yourself.

Never lose your patience—a horse does not reason like you but like a horse!

Never rely on luck and hope for the best.

Never try to place your horse at a jump.

NEVER try to overcome the effects of your wrong seat and lack of training by short cuts. Take your horse back into the manège and start again. It will pay in the end.

As I have explained earlier in this book, the layouts of courses have not progressed but rather returned to what they were like before the war—this is due mainly to the influence of the French National Federation upon the International Federation which is also situated in Paris; I am including here five courses (not used any longer in today's events) because they will make excellent training courses for young horses and young riders. The teachers may reduce these courses by several obstacles if they deem them to be too many. When I drew these courses and laid them out, the system then used was different and in my opinion far more logical than today's way: the riders jumped over those courses only once and then against the clock, while now the number of obstacles has been reduced to some fifteen to sixteen jumps which the riders have to go over twice! I always maintained and still do that it is fundamentally wrong for the following reasons:

(1) If a horse and rider have jumped a clear round in the first leg it stands to reason that the horse should be allowed to rest after a perfect effort and not punished by having to repeat the whole course.

(2) After having gone over the course the first time, horses and riders must often wait for as much as one hour in the cold or heat or rain(!) to start all over again for a second time against the clock.

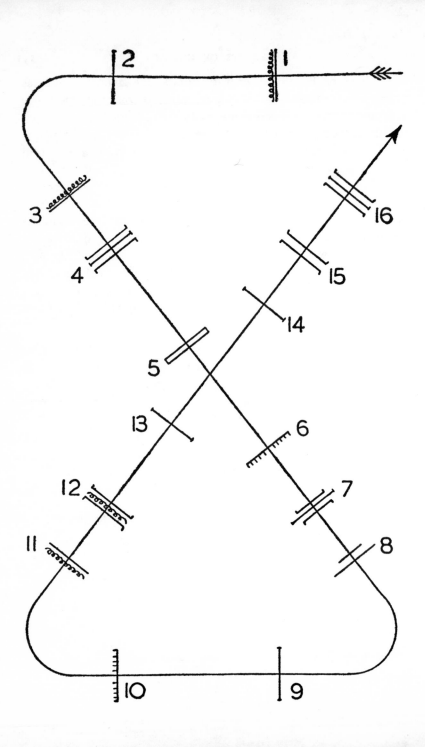

APPENDIX A

COURSE FOR NOVICE RIDERS

Number and Structure of Jumps	Height ft. in.		Width ft. in.		Distance to next Jump feet	strides
1. Brush	3	0	—		70	5
2. Post and Rails	3	3	—		150	12
3. Brush and Rail	3	6	—		35	2
4. Triple Bars	3	9	5	0	70	5
5. Wall	3	6	—		48	3
6. Picket Fence	3	3	—		22	1
7. Hog's Back	3	6	4	6	35	2
8. Double Rustic Gates	3	0	3	0	150	11
and	3	6				
9. Post and Rails	3	3	—		70	5
10. Picket Fence	3	6	—		150	11
11. Brush and Rail	3	3	—		35	2
12. Double Oxer	3	6	5	0	48	3
13. Garden Gate	3	6	—		70	5
14. Post and Rail	3	6	—		35	2
15. Parallel Bars	3	9	4	0	35	2
16. Triple Bars	4	0	6 out			

Total length of Course: 1043   70

This course is composed of 4 combined obstacles and 16 jumps.
Jumps Nos. 3–4 compose Obstacle No. 1.
Jumps Nos. 6–7–8 compose Obstacle No. 2.
Jumps Nos. 11–12 compose Obstacle No. 3.
Jumps Nos. 14–15–16 compose Obstacle No. 4.
Length of the course 350 yards (approx.).
Speed corresponding to such an event 330 yards per minute.
Time limit 1 minute 2 seconds.
Time allowed in the Ring is 2 minutes 4 seconds, but if too many entries this can be reduced to time and a half: 1 minute 33 seconds.

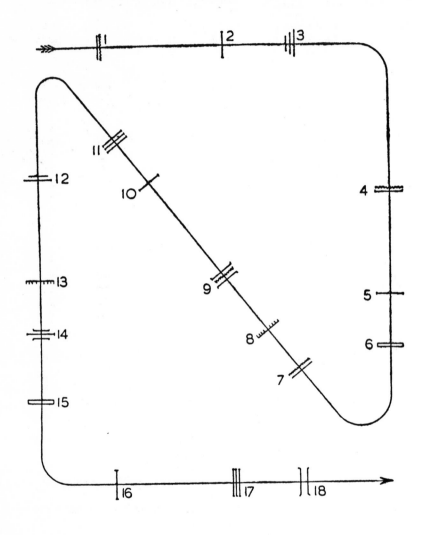

APPENDIX B

COURSE FOR THIRD CATEGORY RIDERS AND HORSES—1

This diagram shows the maximum compactness applicable to such an event. Distances can be lengthened at will, but the correct number of strides must always be taken into consideration.

Number and Structure of Jumps	Height ft. in.		Width ft. in.		Distance to next Jump feet	strides
1. Brush	3	6	—		63	4
2. Post and Rails	3	6	—		36	2
3. Triple Rustic Gates	3	9	4	0	175	13
4. Brush and Rail	3	6	—		50	3
5. Post and Rails	3	9	—		25	1
6. Wall	4	0	—		162	12
7. Brush and Rails	3	6	—		25	1
8. Windsor Gate	3	9	—		37	2
9. Double Oxer	4	0	5	0	63	4
10. Post and Rails	3	6	—		25	1
11. Triple Bars	4	4	6	0	162	12
12. Double Rustic Gate	3	6	4	6	50	3
13. Picket Fence	3	9	—		23	1
14. Hog's Back	4	0	5	0	37	2
15. Wall	4	4	—		162	12
16. Garden Gate	3	8	—		50	3
17. Triple Bars	4	4	6	0	50	3
18. Parallel Bars	4	0	5	0 out		

Total length of Course: 1194   79

This course is composed of 5 combined obstacles and 18 jumps.
Jumps Nos. 2–3 compose Obstacle No. 1.
Jumps Nos. 5–6 compose Obstacle No. 2.
Jumps Nos. 7–8–9 compose Obstacle No. 3.
Jumps Nos. 10–11 compose Obstacle No. 4.
Jumps Nos. 13–14–15 compose Obstacle No. 5.
The length of the course is 400 yards (approx.).
The speed corresponding to such an event 400 yards per minute.
The time limit therefore is 1 minute.
The time allowed in the Ring is 2 minutes, or if there are many entries, only time and a half: 1½ minutes.

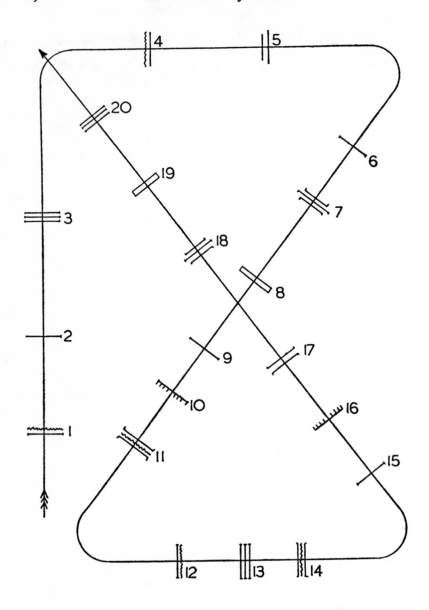

COURSE FOR THIRD CATEGORY RIDERS AND HORSES—2

This diagram shows the maximum compactness applicable to such an event; distances can be lengthened at will but the correct number of strides must always be taken into consideration.

Number and Structure of Jumps	Height ft. in.		Width ft. in.		Distance to next Jump feet	strides
1. Brush	3	6	—		75	5
2. Post and Rails	3	6	—		62	4
3. Triple Bars	4	0	6	0	160	12
4. Brush and Rails	3	6	—		62	4
5. Double Rustic Gates	3	3	4	0	160	12
and	3	9				
6. Garden Gate	3	6	—		37	2
7. Hog's Back	4	4	5	0	51	3
8. Wall	4	0	—		51	3
9. Post and Rails	3	6	—		24	1
10. Windsor Gate	3	9	—		37	2
11. Double Oxer	4	0	5	0	160	12
12. Brush and Rail	3	8	—		36	2
13. Triple Bars	4	0	6	0	26	1
14. Double Oxer	4	0	5	0	160	12
15. Rustic Gate	3	6	—		37	2
16. Picket Fence	3	9	—		37	2
17. Parallel Bars	4	0	5	0	51	3
18. Hog's Back	4	4	6	0	51	3
19. Wall	4	0	—		37	2
20. Triple Bars	4	4	6	0 out		

Total length of Course: 1314   88

This course is composed of 5 combined obstacles and 20 jumps.
Jumps Nos. 6–7 compose Obstacle No. 1.
Jumps Nos. 9–10–11 compose Obstacle No. 2.
Jumps Nos. 12–13–14 compose Obstacle No. 3.
Jumps Nos. 15–16–17 compose Obstacle No. 4.
Jumps Nos. 19–20 compose Obstacle No. 5.
The length of the course is 440 yards (approx.).
The speed corresponding to this event is 400 yards per minute.
The correct time limit therefore is 1 minute 6 seconds.
The time allowed in the ring is 2 minutes 12 seconds, or 1 minute 39 seconds if too many entries.

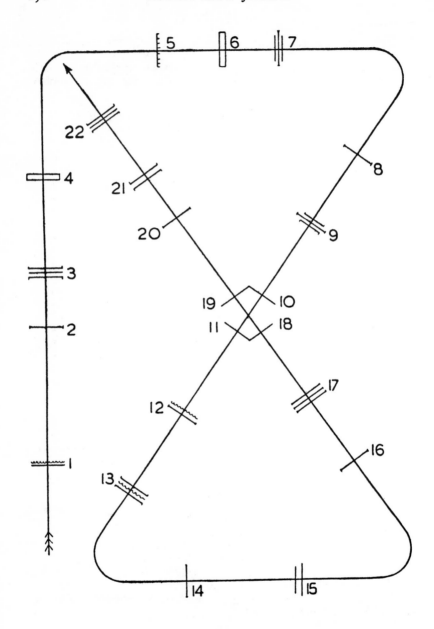

APPENDIX D

COURSE FOR SECOND CATEGORY RIDERS AND HORSES—I

This diagram shows the maximum compactness applicable to such events. Distances can be lengthened at will, but the correct number of strides must always be taken into consideration.

Number and Structure of Jumps	Height ft. in.		Width ft. in.		Distance to next Jump feet	strides
1. Brush	3	6	—		65	4
2. Post and Rails	4	0	—		25	1
3. Triple Bars	4	4	6	0	38	2
4. Wall	4	0	—		170	12
5. Picket Fence	3	0	—		38	2
6. Wall	4	4	—		25	1
7. Hog's Back	4	8	6	0	170	12
8. Garden Gate	4	4	—		53	3
9. Hog's Back	4	4	6	0	53	3
10. Post and Rails	4	0	—		26	1
11. Post and Rails	4	4	—		53	3
12. Brush and Rail	4	0	—		53	3
13. Double Oxer	4	4	6	0	170	12
14. Garden Gate	4	4	—		53	3
15. Double Rustic Gate	4	8	4	6	170	12
16. Post and Rails	4	0	—		65	4
17. Triple Bars	4	4	6	0	53	3
18. Post and Rails	4	0	—		26	1
19. Post and Rails	4	4	—		53	3
20. Gate	4	0	—		25	1
21. Parallel Bars	4	4	5	0	38	2
22. Triple Bars	4	8	6	0 out		

Total length of Course: 1422   88

This course is composed of 5 combined obstacles and 22 jumps.
Jumps Nos. 2–3–4 compose Obstacle No. 1.
Jumps Nos. 5–6–7 compose Obstacle No. 2.
Jumps Nos. 10–11 compose Obstacle No. 3.
Jumps Nos. 18–19 compose Obstacle No. 4.
Jumps Nos. 20–21–22 compose Obstacle No. 5.
The length of the course is 475 yards (approx.).
The speed for such an event is 450 yards per minute.
The speed limit therefore is 1 minute 3 seconds.
The time allowed in the Ring is 2 minutes 6 seconds, or if many entries only 1 minute 33 seconds.

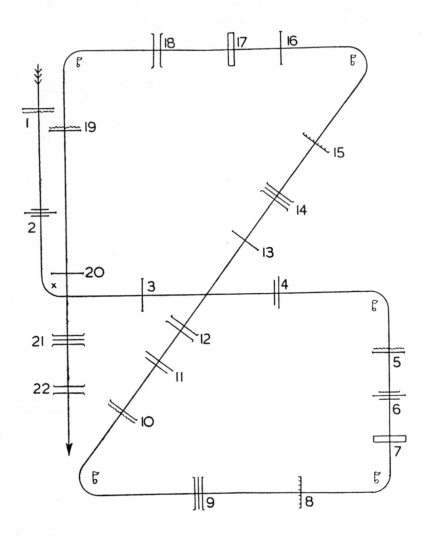

APPENDIX E

COURSE FOR SECOND CATEGORY RIDERS AND HORSES—2

This diagram shows the maximum compactness applicable to such an event. Distances can be lengthened at will, but the correct number of strides must always be taken into consideration.

Number and Structure of Jumps	Height ft. in.		Width ft. in.		Distance to next Jump feet	strides
1. Brush	3	6	—		52	3
2. Hog's Back	4	0	5	0	183	13
3. Post and Rails	4	0	—		65	4
4. Double Rustic Gates	3	8	4	0	183	13
and	4	4				
5. Brush and Rail	4	0	—		25	1
6. Hog's Back	4	4	6	0	25	1
7. Wall	4	8	—		183	13
8. Windsor Gate	4	0	—		52	3
9. Triple Bars	4	8	6	0	183	13
10. Brush and Rail	3	8	—		38	2
11. Double Rustic Gate	3	8	5	0	26	1
and	4	0				
12. Parallel Bars	4	4	5	0	65	4
13. Post and Rails	4	0	—		25	1
14. Triple Bars	4	4	6	0	39	2
15. Picket Fence	4	8	—		183	13
16. Garden Gate	3	8	—		26	1
17. Wall	4	0	—		38	2
18. Double Oxer	4	4	6	0	183	13
19. Brush and Rails	4	0	—		52	3
20. Post and Rails	4	4	—		37	2
21. Triple Bars	4	4	6	0	26	1
22. Parallel Bars	4	8	5	0 out		

Total length of Course: 1689   109

This course is composed of 5 combined obstacles and 22 jumps.
The length of the course is 540 yards (approx.).
The speed corresponding to this event is 450 yards per minute.
The speed limit therefore is 1 minute 10 seconds.
Time allowed in the Ring is 2 minutes 20 seconds, or time and a half; 1 minute 45 seconds; if entries are numerous.

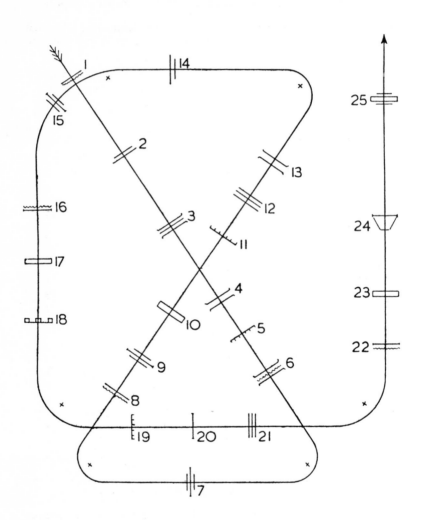

COURSE FOR FIRST CATEGORY AND INTERNATIONAL EVENTS—2

This diagram shows the maximum practicable compactness. Distances can be lengthened at will but the correct number of strides must be taken in consideration.

Number and Structure of Jumps		Height ft. in.		Width ft. in.		Distance to next Jump feet	strides
1. Brush		4	0	—		65	4
2. Double Rustic Gates		4	0	5	0	53	3
	and	4	8				
3. Triple Bars		5	0	6	0	65	4
4. Parallel Bars		4	4	6	0	27	1
5. Picket Fence		4	8	—		27	1
6. Double Oxer		4	6	6	0	184	13
7. Hog's Back		5	0	6	0	184	13
8. Brush and Rails		4	4	—		26	1
9. Hog's Back		4	8	6	0	40	2
10. Wall		5	3	—		53	3
11. Picket Fence		4	4	—		26	1
12. Triple Bars		4	8	6	0	27	1
13. Parallel Bars		4	8	5	0	184	13
14. Double Rustic Gates		4	0	5	0	78	5
	and	4	4				
15. Hog's Back		5	0	6	0	91	6
16. Brush and Rail		4	4	—		27	1
17. Wall		5	0	—		40	2
18. Olympic Gate		5	3	—		184	13
19. Picket Fence		4	4	—		27	1
20. Post and Rails		4	6	—		26	1
21. Triple Bars		4	8	6	0	184	13
22. Brush and Rails		4	4	—		27	1
23. Wall		4	8	—		38	2
24. Liverpool		5	0	6	0	78	5
25. Double Hog's Back		5	0	6	0 out		

Total length of Course: 1661   107

This course is composed of 6 combined obstacles and 25 jumps.
Jumps Nos. 4–5–6 compose Obstacle No. 1.
Jumps Nos. 8–9–10 compose Obstacle No. 2.
Jumps Nos. 11–12–13 compose Obstacle No. 3.
Jumps Nos. 16–17–18 compose Obstacle No. 4.

Jumps Nos. 19–20–21 compose Obstacle No. 5.

Jumps Nos. 22–23–24 compose Obstacle No. 6.

Length of course 555 yards. Corresponding speed 500 yards per minute.

The time limit is therefore 1 minute 6½ seconds.

Time allowed is 2 minutes 13 seconds, or 1 minute 40 seconds if entries are numerous.

INDEX

Compiled by Gordon Robinson